The Poison Fueling My Bloodstream

Diary Entries to Refresh My Soul

Raven Ella Ozlyn

The Poison Fueling My Bloodstream: Diary Entries to Refresh My Soul

© February 2023 Raven Ella Ozlyn

ISBN# 978-1-953526-43-4

Published by TaylorMade Publishing

Jacksonville, FL

www.TaylorMadePublishingFL.com

(904) 323-1334

TaylorMade Publishing

Table of Contents

Introduction

What is the purpose of a diary? To house your most inner person feelings and opinions. Imagine if you got access to a person's diary. That is exactly what this book is about.

Raven Ella Ozlyn is vulnerable to an unknown and infinite audience of people. In this drama and romance book you can count on exploring the inner truth of a young black woman. Who is learning about life through life experiences and forming her own outlook on life. What it means to love and be love? How to differentiate between personal and business? What does she value most in this life?

This book has twist and turns that are worth reading about. This book will make you think even more about this impactful story, and the marvelous mindset of Raven.

Chapter 1: An Older Rendition of Myself

April 9th, 2019

Dear Diary,

A while back, I attempted to start a journal. I do not recall what happened. Well, I do. But this is the actual diary I am going to keep up with. Today was a great day, although I did not get up as early as I wanted.

I got to class on time. My human development class is going well, by the way. I grabbed two hot chocolates for Nana and me from the student union. We agreed the hot chocolate was as amazing as ever.

After class, I went to go see my recruiter, but she was out of town. So, I turned my documents in to the Chief. May I say, "Oh, my!" He is gorgeous. He is handsome. But I did take notice of the amount of hair loss he had on his head. Even still, he was beautiful.

I feel as if I have a dilemma trying to find out who I am. I feel as if I am not being productive enough. I feel like I am being babied too much. I am trying to find my voice. It is so hard with all the different influences.

I want the Lord to shine a bright light on me so that I can be lead in the direction of happiness, which we all know is hard to find. I notice that I always make sacrifices for people, but when I need something, nobody is there to lend me a helping hand. I have noticed this in my friends and my family.

For example, I'm trying to join the Navy. So, eventually, I will have to be shipped off to boot camp. So, I tell my Nana I need her here to watch Hazel (my dog), but her response was "no". I was upset because for the past four months, I've been here in Tallahassee watching her dog. I tell her it's not a problem, but when I asked her to watch my dog, her answer was no.

I think the reason she doesn't want to completely move up here to Tally is because of her boyfriend. He has another two years on his parole, I think. I swear, the day he moves in, I'm going to move out. I dislike that about people. I'm going to start being selfish. Right now, I'm going to focus on stability.

~ R.E.O. ~

April 10th, 2019

Dear Diary,

It is so nice to have someone to talk to. I mean, I talk to my best friend as often as I can, he is amazing. I'm thinking he is the one, but I honestly don't know. I don't want to do a long-distance relationship.

My last boyfriend was a nightmare, so I honestly don't want another one of those. I love my best friend. He is one of the best things that has ever happened to me. I want to be with him, but I honestly don't know what's in the cards for us.

Anyway, today started chaotically. The rental car got towed and we had to get it from the junkyard. It cost one hundred and five dollars because Nana wasn't parked in the visitor's parking spot. Then, I gave her a hundred dollars to extend the car for a week.

My application to join the United States Navy is moving forward and I'm so excited. I don't want to work in retail. I am tired of kissing ass. They promote the wrong people and those customers make me want to pull my hair out. They are so aggravating. Things are looking good for me to leave for boot camp. It's all according to God's plan. Until next time. Night.

~ R.E.O. ~

Dear Diary,

I know I wrote to you earlier, but I just had to write again. I finished my application for the Navy. This is a new chapter in my life. I am making today, the day I officially don't give a care what other people think. I am going to live my life for Raven.

The only person that can make me happy, is me. Forget what everybody else thinks. I need to be seen in a different light because I am not a baby. I am a grown woman. I need to move out and get my place. If I am under my own roof, then nobody can tell me anything. I can be with whomever I want to be with. I can full-heartedly say that on Monday when I get sworn in, I'll be so proud of myself.

The Navy is amazing, so I know I'll be happy. I must stand up to my family and venture out on my own. They treat me like a baby, and I am not. Joining the Navy will give me sustainability and assurance.

Here is the plan:

    1st - pay back student loans and debts

    2nd - build credit, I am going to start with a secured credit card

    3rd - prepare to move out

    4th - get a car.

I am so excited because a few months ago, I was in a predicament that was not in my favor, but this time around, I believe things are going to work out.

~ R.E.O. ~

April 11th, 2019

Dear Diary,

Today was not a productive day. I'm trying to turn my life around and become the person I am meant to be, which is not easy. I don't want to sleep all day, even though it feels so damn good. I got called to go to work today. I hate retail. I cannot wait to quit and do something better. I want some stability and I don't want to have to wait years and years to get it, plus kiss ass along the way. I should start writing poetry to express my emotions and all there is that I hold deep down in my heart. Nevertheless, today is the day I change myself. As of this moment right now, I am reinventing myself for the better.

~ R.E.O. ~

April 24th, 2019

Dear Diary,

Okay, well here's what happened. I went to the Military Entrance Processing Station (MEPS) to take the Armed Forces Vocational Aptitude Battery (ASVAB) test and the physical for the Navy. I did very well, 56 on the ASVAB and I was cleared on the physical. I took a flight by myself from Miami to Tallahassee.

I came back and did a few shifts, well...because I'm broke. Now I must prioritize the little bit of money I do have, even though I will get paid soon. I can't wait to go to boot camp. I have already been enrolled and sworn in. Now, I'm just waiting for the day when I get to go. Everything is genuinely going great, but the one thing I want to talk about is my love life.

I met this guy, and it truly felt like a fairytale. I saw him on the bus but couldn't approach him at that moment. I had messed up my clothes, so, I was extra insecure. Ultimately, I let him get away. I went to class and did everything I had to do. Later on, I got back on the bus and guess who recognized me? We talked for a little bit as I felt him read the nerves all over my face. I felt like this before, but in the past, it was always for a guy that was way out of my league.

I gave him the nickname "Gus" from a Disney movie, and he nicknamed me, "Pixie". He is super fine, tall, about 6'3" and has milk chocolate skin. You know, I love me a chocolate brother. He suggested we meet later that day, but I was so nervous that I said, "I might be busy." By the end of the conversation, I changed my mind and invited him over.

He rode his bike over and we were together about four hours. We talked and shared so much. It indeed was something I could never forget. I think the Lord sent him to me for a reason. All those heartbreaks and sad events disappeared with him. I told him I wanted him and as much as the tension was there, I couldn't have him because he wasn't mine. Yet.

~ R.E.O. ~

May 4th, 2019

Dear Diary,

It is May. I feel like my life is not exactly where I want it to be but getting there. My bank account is in the negative, so I need to get my **S**ugar **H**oney **I**ced **T**ea together. I went to work tonight and let's just say I cannot wait to quit. I tell you, it's just awful. I just want to move on and start my new journey.

Now, let's talk about my love life. Omg! What, love life? I know I don't need a man, but I would really like one. I mean, I crave that love and affection. I think we all do. I also think I most definitely want to love myself first. I mean, I know last time I mentioned Gus, but after a few meet ups, I came to realize; I move too fast. I need to slow down and figure out what a guy needs to have to be ready for me. I'm the one always lending a helping hand to others. People never care about me the way my heart cares about them.

He needs to be financially stable, a Christian, live in his own space, and treat me like the beautiful queen I am. I want a man to love me out of my comfort zone when he drowns me with compliments. I don't believe I'm asking for too much either.

I need to pray to my Heavenly Father and ask Him to lead me in the right direction. I like bus boy. I like my best friend. But the thing is, I am very naive when it comes to love. I'm one of those people that just loves love and believes in fairytales. I do not believe in love at first sight, but I do believe in lust at first sight.

I think the guy that is meant for me is going to be imperfectly perfect. I know I believe in miracles, and I look at the good in everyone, no matter how bad they are or how many red flag they have. I planned to see Gus at 5, but he never responded and that put me in a funk. I know things happen, but now I'm contemplating whether I should see his behavior as a red flag. I already explained to him that he matters. I think I just want to be friends with him right now.

Baby and Hazel, my dogs, are hanging out in front of my bedroom door. I really want to start writing full pages in my diary, and I also want to go enjoy my chips. Should I finish my story or not? ... I will finish it.

I ran into the most disgusting lady. I went to Walmart to get a money order for the rent. I saw this woman let her baby eat bubble gum off the ground at the bus stop. You know, the ground that everyone was walking on! I just want to say this; I would never do that to my future child. Bye Diary.

~ R.E.O. ~

May 29th, 2019

Dear Diary,

I am currently so very grateful for the events that are happening in my life. I love my Heavenly Father. I am so grateful for the Lord blessing me. I love my family. I am deciding to take care of them. I am so happy. I'm planning to move to Miami. I'm pretty sure I want a place with a pool or at least a big yard. We are going to love it. I didn't want to move into this apartment complex I am in, and now I am the only one dealing with the recent infestation.

An old friend named Des, reached out to me recently, he is so ugly, small, and selfish. But anyway, Gus ghosted me because he said we were getting too close. Too bad, I liked him. But I'm at a point in my life where I'm like, "fuck these niggas!" If you are not down for me, then I'm not down for you. I need a man, not a boy. Luckily, I'm seeing Jake. He is my guy friend. I think we would make such a cute couple, and we do. His birthday is the day right before mine. He is fine. I can't wait for us to celebrate together. It's Gemini season, bitch! New career plan, resume, and goals.

~ R.E.O. ~

June 4th, 2019

Dear Diary,

   Today is my second departure meeting, and it is very important. I am meeting a Master Chief, so wish me luck. The event is at noon.

~ R.E.O. ~

September 28th, 2019

Dear Diary,

   It's been a very long time. I honestly don't have an official reason. I guess things were going well once upon a time, and now things are just okay. Well first, I had a great birthday. I went ice skating. I loaned my auntie $400. I feel like things are getting better though. I thought Jake was going to be something new, but I guess not. He lied to me and sugar-coated details, to top things off, he was laughing on the phone like it was all okay. I don't want to give him too much time in my diary. He is irrelevant because he was a loser, and he was not even that cute. He was ugly and just too complicated. I'm officially over him. Going through that situation inspired me to start my YouTube channel, that's about the only good thing that came from the situation. Those weak memories are not what I cherish. Just like I said, I am on a self-love journey. I just want to be myself, live my life and travel.

Here's a question though...what is your idea of perfect happiness?

   My idea of perfect happiness would be to have a job that I like. Probably an FBI agent and I would love to have a business. I want a lover of course, and I want him to not only value my worth, but I want him to want me more than ever before. All the guys I've been with or wanted to be with, I've always ended up wanting them more. I've had more feelings than they did, and I dislike that.

   I know the man that is in store for me is handsome, loyal, and more reliable than any of the other guys whom I've dated, but I've never really had a true boyfriend. I did, however; just find out the truth behind Bobby. He said, "he wasn't that into me." It made me angry because the story he painted begged to differ. Bobby and I are officially not friends. Anyway, I want to be in my own space. I feel like everybody that I trust lets me down. My family, friends, and people in general, they don't look out for me. I'm always left feeling disappointed. It never fails, they always let me down. Not anymore! I am done and I am staying to myself!

~ R.E.O. ~

September 29th, 2019

Dear Diary,

What is your greatest fear? Mine is to never find the love I deserve, oh, and I also fear reptiles. I fear that I may never find the love of my life. In the meantime, I need to fall in love with myself again...or start the process. I don't know what it is. I kind of feel like I need to be by myself. I want to live my life for me. I want to be by myself, have stability and do what I love. I can't trust anyone. Only the Lord and me. He is my savior, and without Him, things would have been a lot worse.

He didn't give me the best parents, but at least I know them. They are alive and well. My mom and dad are just subjects I will have to cover another time. It is only seven-something in the morning right now. I spent a little time with my baby, Hazel, this morning. I love and miss my first dog Jess so much. She is in my heart forever. I feel like I want to detach emotionally from men. I just want to be mean; I am already honest.

I am not going to have a boyfriend until I'm twenty-four, probably. I am young, and I got a lot of growing to do. I am officially dedicated to God and law school. Right now, I am finishing my AA degree, so I can go for my bachelor's degree. I am so excited, but as of now, I don't feel so motivated. I'll be back later today.

~ R.E.O. ~

September 30th, 2019

Dear Diary,

My bad my girl, I did not come back yesterday. I was just down in the dumps. But it's a new day, and I feel alright. Today was better than Sunday. I went to school. After I came home, I tried to pay the rent, but the dumb broad was not there. She made me angry. I just want to slap some sense into her. Anyway, I am going to get it taken care of.

What is the trait you most deplore in yourself?

My trait is my compassion. It's a blessing and a curse at the very same time. I am always there for others, but nobody's there to watch my back. It's so sad because I have a loving heart, I just put too much into everyone and everything. I just don't get it in return. I cannot stress enough how much it gets on my nerves. I know you are supposed to do things for others without expecting something back, but I think common decency is an exception, you know? Until next time.

October 1st, 2019

Dear Diary,

Today I had a departure meeting. It was nice, I met the Senior Chief. He was something else – in a good way. I went to math class and that was good. I was nervous, but things ended up quite nicely. After that, I started my FAFSA. I did not get to the end because I needed my dad's information. Anyway, I am home. I have fed the dogs and myself. I feel like the meeting was a wake-up call that boot camp is not a joke. So, I am glad I got the call today.

What is your greatest extravagance?

My greatest extravagance...I don't have one. I'm tired. I'm going to talk to my best friend and go to bed after. Tomorrow morning, I am going to try a new routine to prepare for boot camp. Goodnight.

~ Future Sailor Ozlyn ~

October 2nd, 2019

Dear Diary,

Today was good. I had a full day of classes, an exam, and a lab report due. I think I am getting better because I am keeping track and giving myself a purpose. I feel like things are looking up. I groomed the dogs a bit today, you know, the usual.

What is your current state of mind?

My current state of mind is...leave me alone! I mean, lately, I've been feeling no sense of what I want. I feel like people are always butting into my life, especially my family. They have too much to say. I think right now in my life, I'm as clear as ever. I want to live my life for me. Period. That's my state of mind. And I'm tired.

~ R.E.O. ~

October 6th, 2019

Dear Diary,

I had a great weekend. I wanted to write every day this month, but I missed a few days. At least I'm persistent, and I keep coming back. That's all that matters. Friday was cool, I did a lot. I made plans for Saturday. It was

FAMU's homecoming and the worst day for me to take the bus. They blocked a lot of streets for the event. I was mad but spent money to go and see the museum, and it was so much fun.

I even ran into an Asian festival. It was not my cup of tea. I grabbed a drink and made my way back home. I forgot the most important thing I did all weekend. I started my YouTube channel. I had so much anxiety, but I'm good now. Things are going great. Tomorrow begins my new diet so I'm excited, you know?

I'm going to answer the million-dollar question for tonight. *What do you consider the most overrated motive?*

I think the most overrated motive is telling a girl what she wants to hear just to get what you want. That's so disgusting and pathetic. You should just be honest and tell her the truth, you know?

~ R.E.O. ~

October 9th, 2019

Dear Diary,

Today was great. I had a full day at school. I came home to a decent house. The dogs are housetrained. My Hazel-Basil and Baby were really in the cage relaxing all day. The dogs wanted me to take them out quickly.

I had Humanities and a paper due today. Thank goodness the professor changed the date because I was not ready. Now, I only have tomorrow to make it work. The chemistry class was great. That annoying guy wasn't there to distract me. I felt smart. American History was alright. Then, I went to Chemistry lab later. The first group changed, which was last week, I was partnered with this group of three white girls. They really made me feel out of place. But this week, working with them was so awkward. We all did the lab. Then, I did have an emergency and Nana had to send me some money. That was super convenient.

The question today is, on what occasions do you lie?

On what occasions can you lie without having to live with the regret of lying? I lie when I need to and when it's in my best interest. For example, when I need something, I say what I need to say to get it. But that's rare. Plus, it is a one-time thing. But I mostly lie to protect the feelings of someone else.

I had a weird dream. I was walking and suddenly I was on a school field. I saw Jake, a guy I was previously dating. He was playing sports with his friends and tried to speak to me. I kept walking. I was smiling, you know I have this habit of giving people the benefit of the doubt when I shouldn't. Proud of myself. I'm happy because this dream signifies me moving on.

~ R.E.O. ~

October 10th, 2019

Dear Diary,

I love when I start on a new page. Right now, I'm texting my best friend. Did I mention him before? He's like my best friend, but the problem is we haven't met before. He is great, but I'm not sure if I'm ready to waste any more time on him. He's not willing to take any chances. The next guy I date is going to be crazy and have fun with me. No questions asked. In other words, he's going to be my best friend.

What do you dislike about your parents?

I don't want to answer this question, but it's so funny. Oh, I watched Lizzo, and she talked about loving yourself. At times, there are some things that I see that make me feel like saying, "okay, I'm not pretty right now." Sometimes I am insecure about my arms, legs, toes, face, skin, hair, and chin. Other times, I feel different, but that's about it. Good night.

~ R.E.O. ~

October 11th, 2019

Dear Diary,

I am back, and it's just to tell you that I am not feeling well. I am not in the mood today, but the day was great. I went to school and had Humanities this morning; I submitted my term paper. I am so proud of myself. I went to chemistry, and of course, the asshole's class, he was giving me a tough time.

Which living person do you most despise?

I feel like this is such an easy question and at the same time, I shouldn't have an answer, but; I do. I still don't like the girls I worked with at Walgreens. I don't like that girl from high school who looked old in the face. I just don't want these people to be in my life any longer. I don't like this other girl that I used to work with at Walgreens, nor her daughter. I just don't like people that have tried to screw me over.

~ R.E.O. ~

October 12th, 2019

Dear Diary,

I am so glad I have someone to talk to. I was very productive today. I woke up early and took the dogs out. I was home and straightened up the house. I cleaned my room and washed my hair. I did not want to post on my channel, so that will have to wait. I went to McDonald's for a McFlurry and also completed an application for the third time. Hopefully, things aren't going to fall through this time around.

I went to the thrift store, came home, and took the dogs out. I made my favorite dinner, salmon, broccoli, and homemade mash. Then, I did some homework and watched one of my favorite movies, *Penelope*. I had a great day. I decided to write before I started studying for boot camp.

My question today is, what is the quality you like in men?

I want to talk about this. I like boys. I've liked boys since the beginning. I just know that I used to say that I don't have a type. I fall for a man's personality, not his looks, but lately I'm attracted to all shades. I like them tall...like the 6-foot ones – they just drive me crazy. I don't mind dreads; I just don't like when they smell bad. A mustache is amazing. I love a sweetheart. I like Melanin. I should write a poem about them. Bye, for now.

~ R.E.O. ~

October 15th, 2019

Dear Diary,

What quality do you like in a woman?

I don't like women, so I'm not going to answer this question. Well, I answered it. I always knew I was straight. I have always liked boys. I love them so much. I'm going to share my poem from yesterday:

I'm into all shades but not all sizes.

I like tall and not 5'5".

Come here, brown eyes, let me take your application.

I don't mind tattoos, but what's the explanation?

He got to work out and not smoke pot.

He got to understand that I am tamed but sometimes wild.

Besides that, he's got to be cute.

Because if it's not obvious, I want you to be my boo.

I want a real man and not a little boy,

I don't want to be toyed with because that's emotional.

Lately, I've been letting the wrong guys in.

So, from now on, you got to fight to apprehend it.

It being my heart

And it's a vessel

So, it's essential.

It's that you be honest from day one about what you plan to be a part of?

I think my poem is great. The day I wrote it, I decided I was glad that I did. I'm not settling for less. No more losers. I want a man and not flings.

~ R.E.O. ~

October 17th, 2019

Dear Diary,

Hey, girl! So you know, I had a one-week break from talking to my best friend. Then, today, I told him that I was done chasing him. He said that he knew that all along. How is that supposed to make me feel? I don't think he's a great friend. I was going to go see him, but for what? He doesn't want to see me; he doesn't want to be with me. I'm re-evaluating what I want in a man.

My love will not settle and wait to decide whether he wants me or not. I dislike it when a guy chases me just to waste my time. I'm always going the extra mile for people, and they give me close to 10% versus the 150% that I give them. That's not fair to me. I have no idea why people act like that. And then they don't understand why I remove them from my life. I'm going to start being blunt with everyone.

Today was a good day. I had a full day at school. I got awarded work-study. Well, I mean, I got the job. I start the study after I get matched. I even took a nap, then walked to McDonald's and then came home. I decided to make tonight a study night.

I'm going to answer the million-dollar question. Which words do you tend to overuse or freeze?

The phrase I use the most is: "that's crazy!", "I know you lying!", "What was it?" And I like to use "well...." when I am being sassy. Well, that's it. Ciao. I got a test tomorrow. Night.

~ R.E.O. ~

October 23rd, 2019

Dear Diary,

I'm not completely sure about the last time I wrote, but today was good. I went to school, and I'm still on a diet. Today I finally got the email to do work-study. Now tomorrow, I get to work. I'm so broke right now. I made a promise to myself to not be broke again. That's my goal. I wrote one of my essays for American History. I'm so proud of myself. I had my Humanities exam today and it was okay. I had a great day in Chemistry. I was so smart.

I like to explain things. So, I'm going to start my YouTube with some of that. I'm going to call it "Not the best workers." and I'm going to do that this weekend. I met a guy this week. His name is irrelevant. I just had to let you know, but I am glad though. I will try not to mention "you-know-who" anymore.

Question: who is the greatest love of your life?

The greatest love of my life...well, I haven't found him yet. But the biggest love has always been me. I love myself. I'm not going to sugarcoat it. I have always loved myself, and there is no way I'm going to lie about that. I'd rather love myself than let others do it. I won't allow my family nor friends to walk all over me anymore. I'm moving forward with me, myself, and I. I'm so excited about this new me.

I asked my family for $20 for my phone bill, they never called me back and ignored all my calls. I'm not mad. I just took note that I am going to learn from this. I want to get my own life. I made the decision a long time ago to get my life in order.

~ R.E.O. ~

November 11th, 2019

Dear Diary,

  I am proud of the amount of time I have written to you. After tonight, I'm going to try to write every day this week. But girl, yesterday I met up with this boy. It was awful. I can say it here. He's from Broward, and he's trifling. First, he was very persistent. I told him I didn't want to meet. He wanted me to travel to him. He didn't want to make the trip to meet me. Then, when we met, he wanted me to call him an Uber to his home because he noticed that I took an Uber. And to top everything off, he's pansexual. I'm not offended. I just don't see anything but a friendship.

  Anyway, we met up in front of this clothing store. Then, we started walking. He was persistent about trying to come over to my place. He was doing too much. I was thinking about going to McDonald's, but he didn't have any money. He wanted me to buy him a drink and food. I was like, "Okay, let's go." We walked, and he was inconsiderate. He wanted me to walk him back to his street. So, he can walk 20 minutes home, and I would have to walk 40 minutes. He is such a little BITCH! The icing on the cake was when he asked to borrow my phone.

  When he borrowed my phone, he signed me out of my Facebook and logged into his. He legit spent 20 minutes on my phone. Those were just a few of the red flags that popped up. He was terrible. Cancel! I don't want to hang out with him again. I'm going to be busy whenever he asks me what I'm doing. He kept asking me questions, and I didn't like it.

  Anyway, I'm trying to write my book, save some money and do my own thing. I'm seeing somebody. He is okay. I don't know about him because I will be leaving for the Navy soon. I'm just not sure.

~ R.E.O. ~

December 23rd, 2019

Dear Diary,

  I've been away for a while I know, but I promise you, I've been on my grind. This semester a lot of things have been happening. Things should be moving into place, and I can't wait for it. I had a counseling session that went well. School is okay and I'm ready to end it. I noticed that the people in my American History class stopped conversing with me. They are full of shit. I'm not surprised because that's just what white people do. It's cool; I stand by myself, and...that's more than fine. I kind of wish I had a friend that was as good of a friend to me as I am to them. I would keep in contact with that person for as long as I could.

I broke things off with Des. He was playing games. I look back at the situation about calling Des and letting him know I'm not mad. Well, next week is Thanksgiving. I'm so excited. I get to go home to see my family.

The million-dollar question today is, what talent would you most like to have?

The answer is to play an instrument that I've always wanted to learn, the violin, the piano, and perhaps even the cello. I have tried, but I just couldn't get it. I'm going to try again someday.

~ R.E.O. ~

Dear Diary,

I've been working at McDonald's for a few weeks now. Things are okay. I'm going to be there for a few more weeks, so I'm not worried. Things are going according to plan so far and I am grateful. This is going to be my last debt meeting, so I am free for Christmas. I'm so happy. So far, I have two good friends, Emily, and Nydia. They haven't been anything but good to me.

I'm not going to lie; I've been procrastinating. I need to pull through for math and chemistry. I know I have the energy. I just need to dig deep. I tried this new scholarship app called Mos. I paid a dollar to get started. Today's been great so far and I'm excited. Not being friends with my best friend has worked out great. I feel like he was a waste of time and energy, honestly. What I was looking for was a counselor. I like the free sessions at school. I feel like I'm going to continue in the future. I love that it helps me sort my thoughts and grief and gives me free space.

My million-dollar question today is if I could change one thing about myself, what would it be?

I believe the answer would be my mindset/opinion about myself. I am beautiful and blessed. The love of God has made me happy and healthy. Everything else that I've ever wanted, the Lord has blessed me with. I cannot and I do not have the right to complain or be ungrateful. I just pray that the Lord makes me blessed, loving, and spiritually whole. Give me all the tools, my Lord, that I may need to continue to be covered in the blood of Jesus. Amen.

> I cannot and I do not have the right to complain or be ungrateful.

~ R.E.O. ~

December 1st, 2019

Dear Diary,

Today is December 1st. My plan is so close to being completed. I did not go to work at McDonald's. I got in town from the Greyhound at 11:30 PM. I went home and had to clean up my dog's mess. It had to be done. I know that when I go to Mickey D's later, they will raise hell and have a fit for me missing work, but that's okay. I'm about to put in a two-week notice. I am so excited and tired.

I'm currently listening to Christmas music and writing to you. I might take a nap before I get started. I got to hit a home run to end this semester, of course. I'm so excited I have a busy week ahead. I love it. I am proud of myself. I feel like I never admit it to myself. I love me so much. I am a beautiful, loving, and strong black woman in this society where the color 'white' is as powerful as it gets. Last night, my Uber driver was drunk as hell, and I think he was racist.

I also found out my dad went to jail last night. He was selling drugs – how could he ever allow himself to do something so irresponsible? He gave my Nana $500. I hope he's okay. I love my dad. I mean, I only have one set of parents. I just want the best for not only Nana, but everyone in general.

I went back home for Thanksgiving break, which was very nice overall. Nana leaves to go back home in 10 days. I love my Nana. She is going to take my grandma and my great grandma to the hospital. She is awesome. We are going to go get breakfast from Krispy Krunchy Chicken later in the week. I can't wait. I got Hazel. Today was the first time I was shopping at Piggly Wiggly. It was okay.

The million-dollar question now is, what do you consider to be your greatest accomplishment?

I would say staying true to myself. I love school, and no matter the circumstances, I have a plan to find myself.

~ R.E.O. ~

December 2nd, 2019

Dear Diary,

My legs are extra tired. Today was cool. I missed Humanities, but I went to Walmart with my Nana. I got my agenda that I wanted to start the new year. I also made it back to go to chemistry. Our chemistry teacher is great, so I'm not worried.

I got breakfast for Nana and me. We had the honey chicken biscuit sandwich and hot chocolate. I went to class, came back, and then I dropped Nana off to go to her appointment by Lyft. She was complaining about the price, but she made it. I have to get my 2018 college information for her.

About American History, I got my paper back and I saw that I got an 88, and I'm not mad at it. Then, I went and worked on science and math later. Stephen and I were partners for the assignment that was due tonight. I mainly did everything, but Stephen came through and helped a lot. Things wrapped up nicely. I'm proud of this accomplishment that's nearly complete. I am excited.

~ R.E.O. ~

December 3rd, 2019

Dear Diary,

I'm like extra-freaking tired tonight. I had a long and busy day. It was productive...for the most part. This morning, I wanted to write about my dream last night. I was hanging out with a guy. I went into a room; I looked back and he wasn't there. I was really upset. How could I let it happen again? I like him, I just don't like the way he handled the situation. The school was great. I have a DEP meeting tonight. I feel quite motivated. Wish me luck!

~ R.E.O. ~

December 4th, 2019

Dear Diary,

I am so excited I have spent five consecutive days working. I don't plan on messing up either. Today went well. I'm wrapping up the semester nicely. I just have to finish strong in chemistry. Now, about American History and Humanities, I feel good about them because Humanities is no biggie. I befriended a guy, and he is a history major. When I studied by myself, I didn't do so well, so he gave me a copy of his study guide.

The nicest thing Nana did today was my laundry and she also cooked me dinner. Plus, she helped me with the dogs. I wrapped up chemistry. I feel great about moving forward.

~ R.E.O. ~

December 11ᵗʰ, 2019

Dear Diary,

    I know I tried to write every day this month. But you know what? Elena from the Vampire Diaries didn't. Other than that, I've just been busy between Nana and my responsibilities. I have been finishing up working, trying to stack my money for when I plan on leaving and I got accepted to BVU!!! Yass girl!!! I'm so excited. I'm going to be traveling and getting my bachelor's from wherever I am. Next year is going to be so much better.

    I'm always covered in the blood of Jesus. He is my flashlight, for he leads me in the right direction. He has always been doing it, so, I have no worries about the future. I know he's going to put me where I need to be and not where I want to be. I love my Heavenly Father, and I thank him for keeping my family safe and happy. The Lord is continuing to watch over us all. My final for Chemistry and American History is on Friday. I am about to study my ass off!

~ R.E.O. ~

Chapter 2: Die With Memories, Not Dreams

My name is Raven Ella Ozlyn, but for some weird reason, people call me "Ell." I guess it is catchier. I'm from Florida, and I am in the United States Navy. I have been in for almost two years. I get asked a lot about the reasons relating to why I joined the Navy, and my answer is always the same, "I joined to find a better version of myself."

I grew up sheltered. I went off to a university right after high school graduation – well, not right away; I had to wait 6 months for the Spring semester to start. I was slaving at Walgreens for eight dollars and twenty-five cents an hour until then. I believe terrible things happen in waves of three. The first semester was a disaster – going into the summer of that year. Everything that I wanted and worked for had fallen apart. As I stated, I believe bad things happen in threes:

(1) I lost my seven-thousand-dollar four-year scholarship because my grades slipped

(2) I lost my first apartment because it was inhabitable

(3) And I lost my first puppy (Jessie). I just couldn't make it work.

In a nutshell, I moved back home with Jess, my dog. The next day I arrived in town; Jess passed away. I rushed her to the vet because she was not able to stand – something was seriously wrong with her internally; I had sensed it. The general examination concluded that her lungs were collapsing. She had been poisoned by the friend I was staying with at the time.

She was in a lot of pain, and I just could not see her like that. So, to ease the right of passage, to soften her journey from this world to the next, I paid for Jess to be put down and cremated. I held her in my arms as I saw and felt the life inside her fade away. By far, it was one of the most devastating things I had to go through in my entire life. I cried my eyes out for three days straight. To this day, I still tear up at the videos and photos I have of her. I believe that a person moves on from another person, yet; never truly moves on from a dog, let alone their first.

I needed another thing to pour all my love into, so what do I do? I buy another puppy. Jess was a Blue nose Pit Bull. This time around, I bought a Red nose Pit Bull and named her Hazel. I made sure I sued my apartment complex. I was awarded all my money by the county. I mentioned that she was poisoned by the friend I was staying with at the time and now I know that person was not my friend.

As I think back, I feel as if I should have moved back when my family told me to. I just didn't want them to be proven right, to have them feel that I had failed. Or at least, I wanted to call it "quits" when I was ready – not on anybody else's terms. I know I am stubborn. It is one of my favorite traits. It helps me make the right decisions and make the right moves when needed.

Later in the year, I moved to Tallahassee. I found myself in a big and spacious three-bedroom apartment. I went to Tallahassee Community College. I was putting the pieces of my life back together. Finally! At the end of each night I was also alone. I decided to get my associate degree and join the Navy at the end of the year. I crossed the line from civilian to active military and I've been looking forward ever since.

I graduated from Boot Camp on March 13th, 2020 – it was one of the proudest, happiest moments of my life. It sucked because my family couldn't be there. The Covid-19 virus had come about, therefore; plenty of shutdowns were in effect all over and travel bans. My family did have a watch party and was able to watch it on Facebook live. I went to A School and I settled in. After a while, my Nana sent me my diary with a few other things. I just continued to document my life and write very often as I had done before.

Anyway, I'm just currently thinking about everything. My current situation and all the incompetent people I'm surrounded by. It's funny because I left home to live life and be a part of something bigger than me. I find myself alone and in a bigger shit show than before. Since the beginning of deployment, I talked to my friend, Kayla. I told her everything that was going on. She kept saying that my life on the ship could be a whole reality show. I was constantly in agreement with her. Then, the crazy idea kept rolling in my mind. Why not check off my bucket list item to write a book?

This book is based on anyone who would ask me, "*how was your deployment?*" This book would be my answer. Of course, I would keep in mind privacy and that sort of thing. I'm going to imagine my Naval career was in an alternate universe or dimension. Names and titles altered; I'm going to give you the full story. I promise you; I cannot fabricate any of the material. The book events are based on real events, and some things will be sugar-coated. To certain people, things may seem familiar, or they may even recognize the story. I've officially concluded that I don't care. In addition, if they choose to identify themselves or correct anything, they can leave a review.

I think I deserve this book. They say you are supposed to kill people with kindness. Or you beat them with success. Why not use this as a platform to start my career as an author? I am a very passive person. I say, "It is okay," when a lot of times it is not okay. I let people get away with a lot. Once you cross that line of no return – it is just that – there is no fucking redemption to be found, no way out. I have all this bottled-up anger, and I just need a positive breather, and this is it. This is my sigh of relief.

Well, to tell you the full story, I need to start from the very beginning. I arrived at my first ship right after finishing A School in Great Lakes, IL. The school was great. I knew one of my A School buddies (Fred) would eventually join me on the ship. He just had to go to a C School first. I took a leadership position. I kept the records of everyone in my class. I didn't do it in boot camp, so I tried the position. It was a fun time. I love school; it was just a problem here and there at the barracks (living space). Another story for another time. Well, let me elaborate.

When I was first assigned my room, I had one roommate, Carly. She was amazing. We hung out and cleaned our room for inspection together – two proud black sisters one may call it. Then, we got assigned 3 more roommates. It all went downhill from there. This one girl, Rachel, was something else. She got caught on the male floor and got in trouble. She lost her orders to go to Hawaii. The next thing I knew, the two of us didn't get along after that. I don't remember what happened exactly. I do remember she came at me very disrespectfully and got in my face. I snapped back, used the word 'bitch', but I didn't call her a 'bitch'. She then, tried to get tough and get in my face again. Oh, hell no! I couldn't with her.

Another issue was that this girl came into our room at almost 1 a.m., drunk as a skunk. She was friends with the three new girls who had moved in. She came in and was talking to my rack mate. Mind you, it's pitch black in the room, everybody was sleeping, it's bunk beds and I'm on the bottom bunk. She scared the shit out of me. I was upset and ended up reporting that incident. She was standing in front of me while I was sleeping, talking to nobody. After a couple more incidents, I moved rooms. I got to move in with my friend at the time, Alicia.

I moved in, and everything was cool at first. A couple of weeks later, Alicia tried to pull a fast one over on me. Mind you, I was about to leave in three weeks. I had a duty-free weekend, so I was chilling. She had a double watch, plus she found out she was going to Japan. And that meant she wasn't leaving A School for six months. One Sunday, we were both relaxing in the room and this was the exchange:

"I'm about to go get some Pizza Hut and go to the supermarket. Do you want something?" I asked Alicia. "No," she replied. I left and I came back in a while. As soon as I entered the room, she asked me about my fishtail makeup brushes. "Yea," I responded, "They were a gift from my mom." The next thing she said was, "I don't believe you; I know you stole my makeup brushes." I thought she was joking because:

1) if you were missing something, why would you wait until Sunday to say something about it? She never mentioned anything about ordering makeup brushes the whole week, let alone the weekend.

2) They were a gift, and I didn't have the complete set, plus they were used. I never did my makeup at A School. I just cleaned them, and they were stained. When I cleaned them, my last roommate Carly, said, "Those are cute." I asked my Nana to send me my makeup bag a while ago. Those were in my possession for the longest.

3) She went through my dresser when I wasn't in the room. If she was missing something, why didn't she just ask me? I would have given her the same answer. I replied, "You went through my stuff and stole from me."

I called my auntie because I was about to slap the shit out of her. She disrespected my auntie, and my auntie wanted to beat her ass too. The situation was making me angry. Why would I steal a twenty-dollar pack of makeup brushes? They were more like six dollars on Wish. I had just bought a $1500 laptop and I just bought a $200 pair of Air Pods. I was a Seaman; she was a seaman recruit. I said, "I make more money than you!" Her whole story did not make sense; it still doesn't today.

We went to the NMTI, and we brought the issue for the make-up brushes. Long story short, it was decided that I would change rooms. When I reflected on the situation, I realized that she was jealous and miserable. It was May when the incident happened, and she wasn't leaving until November. I was leaving in less than 30 days. When I told my friend Foxtrot about it, she said, "That big lip bitch!" That was the highlight of the conversation, and it made me laugh the whole thing off.

It didn't turn out too bad. It worked out great. I moved in with three lovely ladies, and they always had this great motto – "Cause a pussy hoe could never." They were super funny. We all eventually left and continued with the next chapters of our Naval careers.

"Cause a pussy hoe could never."

~

March 15th, 2020

Dear Diary,

This Corona virus is creating madness. Everything is shutting down. It seems like the plot in a movie about something where the world ends. It sucks. I feel sick with my dry cough, especially around this time. I hope it clears up. I got some NyQuil to help. I finished with boot camp, so glad. I'm excited to be going forward in my career.

My clothes are in the washer, and we got to go out. I am tired. But the fight is not over. I know that I just have to continue to keep pushing and swim to the finish line. I am so glad to be out of boot camp and officially be a sailor. It is so surreal. I am super proud of myself. I love you so much. Today, I woke up early to muster, but I am on base liberty. So, I took a nap, then went to Taco Bell and grabbed tacos. Now, I'm back in my dorm and watching Netflix. The next step is to sit back and relax.

~ R.E.O. ~

March 17th, 2020

Dear Diary,

Tomorrow, I need to buy a new phone. I don't want to buy it, but I have no choice. It is a lot of work to tell all my contacts about my new number! I can't leave, everything is on lockdown. I'm not about to rush it, plus I have a bad cough now. I don't want any problems. Anyway, I am glad to be out of boot camp. I am a sailor. I can't wait to be connected. No more payphone for me. Currently, I am still in INDOC. I know I'm going to be on hold for a while and I don't mind.

~ R.E.O. ~

March 18th, 2020

Dear Diary,

Today was good. I went to class and learned a lot about savings and money. I am still upset I need to go and get a new phone, but I have no choice with the widespread virus and the increasing deaths – more and more as each day passes. I am living restricted. Nothing is open but, at least the PRT is canceled for this training group.

I can't wait to call my Nana. I miss my family so much. But I'm growing up, so I will be more independent than I already am. I like it here.

The simple shit is lame to do, but to be a part of the best is worth it. I love the training at the moment. I am here, so everything is worth it!

~ R.E.O. ~

March 20th, 2020

Dear Diary,

I am working hard on being better financially. I am tired. I had two watches yesterday. I'm tired of lunch at the galley...#BudgetLife. I am trying to do better financially – so far, so good. Setting myself up for success. And I love every second of it. Just trying to do my best.

I need the Lord to help me and keep me in his shadows with the Holy Spirit. I love my Heavenly Father. He comes to me and shields me from evil. He continues to show me that I am strong. That's why I'm trying to be the best. The Lord has shown me what needs to be seen now. I know he will keep me, and my family covered. There are no worries here. In Jesus' name, I pray. Amen.

~ R.E.O. ~

March 26th, 2020

Dear Diary,

I haven't written in a while, but I like writing. It helps me catch up with my thoughts because I swear, I'm in a stop-and-slap-a-bitch mode. I hate the situation that happened with Alicia, but I feel good writing about it. I hate phony females. This bitch is fake. I loathe this bitch. I need my real diary.

~ R.E.O. ~

April 16th, 2020

Dear Diary,

I have missed you so much. The last time I wrote, I was a civilian. Now I am an active-duty service member. I am so proud. Graduation was March 13th. It would have been great, but because of Corona there were no guests, no Liberty and everything was closed. Mail has been taking forever to come, but I'm not complaining. Soon everything will be back to normal, hopefully. I'm so glad to have you back. I'll write to you later, love.

~ R.E.O. ~

April 22nd, 2020

Dear Diary,

I know my real diary came in the mail a while back. I am wrong for not writing. I apologize, but girls be playing with me. I have to stay guarded here. They had me messed up. But that situation is over. I'm in a new room with my new roommate. No drama. They are cool so far, but you know, I don't want to jinx it. There has been a turn of events in the "Dirty Jersey". Instead of the 11 people that we normally have, now there are 17, and these girls act like it's a surprise.

I like writing to you because you make me calm. I'm going to rethink which school I want to go to. Hopefully, tomorrow I will get my orders, and hopefully, they say Spain. So far, I have been practicing my Spanish. I'm so happy to be in the military, to finally be a part of something bigger than myself.

I thank God for everything and for always being my protector. I'm thankful. I'm going places, and I'm thankful to be covered in the blood of Jesus. He gets me every time, my Lord, and my savior. And so, in Jesus' name, I pray. Amen. I love the tap song. It's beautiful. I'm ready for the real thing, but I'm sticking to God's plan.

~ R.E.O. ~

April 26th, 2020

Dear Diary,

I saved this fat ass page to write to you, and guess what? I am late. I got my orders on Friday, and I'm just now writing on Sunday to tell you that we are going to Virginia Beach. Like holy shit, I am so freaking ready! It's only the beginning; I was stunned that it didn't say Spain, but I know that the Lord has a plan in store for me. I am doing so great right now. I'm listening to Bruno Mars and just chilling right now. I talked to my aunties and my nana, but I should probably tell my mom and dad. I don't like people all up in my business.

I'm also so proud of myself and the only person I can give thanks to is Jesus Christ. He protects and continues to cover me in His blood. For this protection and to continue to guide me, I love Him. He is my Holy Father. Today is a beautiful Sunday, and I freaking love it. He has led me here and this place and predicament for a reason. He's showing me the right ways to grow up. I love Him so much. I praise His name, and I feel like I need to pray more. That's one thing that I am going to pray and work on. We need our one-on-one conversations. I pray that the Lord continues to bless my family and me. Thank you, my Lord!

~ R.E.O. ~

April 28th, 2020

Dear Diary,

It's not that I am failing or anything in school. I just want to be at the top of the class. Right now, I am up there but not up there. So disappointing. I need to do better – like a hundred times better, a hundred percent more. So far, I only have 100%, 97%, and a 98%, but overall I'm proud of myself. I am a bit annoyed today. I'm tired, so I will go and take a shower, order some things off Wish, and call it a night. Thirty more days left, and it is not bad at all. I love you. Night, love.

~ R.E.O. ~

May 5th, 2020

Dear Diary,

I am halfway through A School. I'm leaving and shipping out to Virginia Beach. Life is great. I wanted to write sooner. I finally traded in my boot camp shower shoes and got a new pair. I got me some Nike sandals. I'm pretty sure I need to break them in, but they look great. I just need to grab myself a pair of Converse and I'll be good. Tomorrow is my sister's birthday.

~ R.E.O. ~

May 20th, 2020

Dear Diary,

I love writing and expressing things to you – so far, so good. I am in A School. I just finished working out. At least 30 push-ups and 30 sit-ups. I'm so proud of myself. I love what God has in store for me. Just the fact that He continues to make way for my family and me is enough for me to keep going. I love him so much.

I know my Nana doesn't want me to worry about the whole housing thing, but I do. But I am not worried. I gave it to God. He will protect us and cover us in the blood of Jesus. My Heavenly Father that I praise and worship. My favorite song is "Father, can you hear me?" from the Tyler Perry movie. He continues to give me strength. I love him so very much. I need to start praying every night. I am very grateful. I wanted to continue with school. But I have no choice but to put it on hiatus and wait for what's in store for me.

For the Lord, I pray that you continue to bless me. I hope you bless me with a godly husband. I haven't met him. And I have no idea what he looks like. I pray that he enters my life at the right time. I pray that we are in love and praise our Heavenly Father. I pray that you continue to bless my family and friends. Please continue to watch over my mother. I know what she has done, and it is not godly. But please, continue to have a conversation with her and bless her. But I pray that you guide her in the right direction.

We are never too old to learn from our mistakes and learn how to praise you. I'm still learning myself. Please protect my brothers and sisters. Thank you for blessing my auntie with a beautiful daughter. Today was her birthday. I wasn't there physically, but I was there spiritually. I used to think only of Sunday as a worshipping day. But I was wrong; every day is worshiping day. Today was also my shipmate's birthday; happy birthday to her. Next month will bring my birthday. I am grateful to have a great career. With the love and support from my family, I could've never made it this far. I love everyone; I love every ounce of it.

I beat myself up about not having a companion and I have to continue to realize that I give myself all this love before I expect somebody else to do it – to pull me together. Because I have nothing to worry about, for I am blessed. I'm listening to Charlie Wilson. I am blessed. My other sister's birthday came and went, and I just told her happy birthday. She got a car for her birthday. I didn't feel any way about it. I know I work hard for everything I have and I take care of it because nothing was given to me. I have to go. I want to go my way and to be perfectly candid, it's much, much better this way. It's a beautiful feeling when you've worked hard by yourself to earn something. I'm happy for my sister, and I pray that she is safe on the road. God bless her.

~ R.E.O. ~

May 17th, 2020

Dear Diary,

Today is a rainy day. I went and got Dunkin' Donuts for lunch and Panda Express for dinner. I'm going to have a spa day. My duty-free weekend is great. I'm sad it is coming to an end.

~ R.E.O. ~

I downloaded this motivational app on my phone. I love this app with a passion. This is my first quote:

"The only thing standing between you and your goal is the bullshit story you keep telling yourself as to why you can't achieve it."

~ Jordan Belfort ~

I think quotes are my form of coping. They are so real. There is always a quote to make you think and get through whatever it is you're going through. I decided to read a quote every day and ponder about it and try to do better and apply it to myself as much as possible.

May 20th, 2020

"Sometimes, life will kick you around, but sooner or later, you realize you're not just a survivor. You're a warrior, and you're stronger than anything life throws your way."

~ Brooke Davis ~

Dear Diary,

Today is a bittersweet day. My roommates left to go to the fleet. I wish I got to spend more time with them. But I'm grateful for the time I did get to spend with them. I am extra glad. I leave in eight days...

I also got my lowest grade today – 88%. I am so upset. I love that I am learning my job...

I got another fortune cookie. I know the guy I'm talking to is not the one...

I might go visit an old friend. Who knows? I'm working on things. Hopefully, things will go smoothly for me. Night!

~ R.E.O. ~

~ Later that day ~

I was highly excited when my diploma for my Associate's from Tallahassee Community College arrived. My Nana sent me a picture, and I was just super proud of myself. Nothing can stop me! I have and will continue to excel in life!

~ R.E.O. ~

May 22ⁿᵈ, 2020

Dear Diary,

I had to work and overall it was an okay day. I was aggravated, but I called my crazy auntie. That was good because everything worked out okay. I also talked to my Nana. I love my family. They are lovely. They make me feel better. I am going to take one week of leave rather than two weeks. If I take two, then I will be in the negative. I think one week of leave will be more than enough time to spend with them. I'm excited only six days left.

~ R.E.O. ~

May 23ʳᵈ. 2020

"Starting today, I need to forget what's gone. Appreciate what remains and look forward to what's coming next."

~ M. A. ~

I think this quote reminded me of my barracks incident. It could also remind me that my naval career was officially about to begin. That was just a pregame version for the real main event. I was more than ready to start the next chapter in my life.

~~~~~~

Dear Diary,

I know I should be enough, but I keep longing for a companion. I want to love, to be loved. I want a healthy relationship, of course. I'm going to wait my turn, but still, I am grateful. I know I must work on one thing at a time. First, I'm trying to clean up my credit score and pay off some debt. I am hoping for the second round of stimulus checks, so I can put a grand with my savings to pay it off. Then I don't have to be bothered by it anymore. I know I want my credit to go up. I am going to buy a car and I'm going to get a credit card. I just want to be the best version of myself. I can accomplish anything. I love Jesus. I pray he continues to bless me and my friends and family.

~ R.E.O. ~

May 30ᵗʰ, 2020

"We may have all come on different ships, but we're in the same boat now."

~ Martin Luther King Jr. ~

I graduated from A School on May 30th, and I graduated top five. I was so excited to leave Chicago, Illinois. I never got the opportunity to explore any of it because of COVID. I wanted to try this place called CYOC – an acronym for Create Your Own Cheesecake. I pray one day I get the opportunity to explore and indulge my curiosity in the future.

I arrived in Virginia the next day after graduating from A School. Before I could board my ship, I had to be quarantined in a hotel for two weeks. I ended up staying a week longer because I got sick. I did not have COVID, but I did have similar symptoms. I had the worst headache for a couple of days, I felt terrible. They did send me to get COVID tested because of my other symptoms. That worked out well because they wanted me to move all my things on a temporary ship for a week before I moved onto my ship. That sounded like way too much work. Until next time!

~ R.E.O. ~

June 3rd, 2020

Dear Diary,

I have no idea why I did not write on May 29th, 30th, or the beginning of June. At least the first of the month. Anyway, I graduated from my A School. So glad I am no longer in Chicago. That same day I did buy a car from my cousin. Long story short, I do not have that car anymore. I'm perfectly fine because all that money goes back into my savings. In addition, the car that I do end up getting in the future will be just for me. The internet keeps going in and out. So far, everything is good. I did a bad thing last night. I thought about doing it again tonight. Other than that, I can't wait for my birthday. I just want to get my hair done and eat at my favorite restaurant, Chili's. I want to get dolled up, but I can't, and it sucks.

~ R.E.O. ~

June 15th, 2020

Dear Diary,

Now we are in June. Halfway through the year. I am stuck in a hotel and cannot go anywhere. How about my birthday is on Thursday? I can't celebrate it, though. I did ask a friend of mine to buy me some cupcakes and Popeyes. It doesn't matter. Last year I had so much fun on my birthday and I spent time with my loved ones. This year, I am spending it by myself in a hotel room that I cannot get out of. I cannot believe this. Everything happens for a reason though, I'm not mad. I just wish I could go do something or have something special.

~ R.E.O. ~

June 18th, 2020

"Remember, when you forgive, you feel. And when you let go, you grow."

"Remember, when you forgive, you feel. And when you let go, you grow.

~ Anonymous ~

I think this quote reminded me of my mom. When I left for boot camp, everyone – friends and family – filled me with their personal opinions about the military. However, they all wished me the best of luck in my Naval career. Just one person did not have the nicest things to say to me, that was my mother. My second to last time seeing my mom, she said, "I don't think you are going to make it in the Navy. I don't think you are going to make it through boot camp. You are a cry-baby. A big bag of water." Then, she started laughing about it with her boyfriend. I didn't say anything at that moment, but she hurt my feelings. Thanks, mom!

Even if that was how she felt, why would she count on my downfall? Boot camp was difficult for me. It took me six weeks to learn how to swim. I couldn't march for anything. I hated running and that 1.5-mile run was either going to make or break me. I had to pick myself up a lot and depend only on God. I could only reach out to my family twice in ten weeks. I remember when I was knocked down, I thought about what she said. The tears just started flowing. I felt like a cry-baby. Even if I am one, I never let anyone see me cry. Only a handful of people get to see my ugly, crying face. The lip quivers, the puffy eyes, the snot rockets. Only a few people get to see such a beautiful work of art.

After I graduated from boot camp, I was in A School. I sent my mom a letter in the mail. It explained how I felt and how I did not like the words she said to me. I wanted her to acknowledge the hurtful message she gave me and left it in my heart. I ended the letter by saying I did not want her to call or text me, that I wanted her to write me a letter back. I was completely flabbergasted when I received her letter in the mail the following week. When I received a letter with my mother's name on it, I instantly took a deep breath and opened it. The card and letter read as follows:

"Congratulations on your graduation! To view every day as a learning adventure with brand new ideas to explore, to know that the worthwhile achievements you make will eventually lead to more... To live a full life in the way that you've chosen. Refusing to settle for less, take on your destiny, and build your dreams. This is to be a success. Hope you feel pride in this achievement and excitement for the new possibilities ahead."

"Ms. Raven Ella Ozlyn, "2020"

You did it, baby! Mommy is so proud of you. Your whole family is praying for you. Keep going, baby! Never give up!"

~ The letter included with the card ~

3/2/2020 11:33 pm

Dear Ms. Ozlyn,

Mommy misses you so much. I've received my letters and your beautiful, strong pictures! I am so proud of you, baby. You had your mind made up to do it, and you did it. Baby, I want to apologize for hurting you in any way that I have. "You're not a cry-baby." Baby, you're a "strong, black, beautiful woman!" The woman I'm so proud of, as a matter of fact, is the strongest woman I know. I want you to be able to talk to me about anything, baby. Anything! I've never looked down on you because you always made me proud! I'm so sorry, baby. I'm crying. When you left home, I think I cried all that week. Not because I thought you wouldn't make it, but because I was scared. That's just a feeling mothers go through. I'm always feeling scared, scared that something just might happen. I even have panic attacks worrying about my daughters...

I miss you so much. I just keep looking at your pictures. Your grandmother is jumping for joy up there, saying, "my baby made it!" I can't wait to see you! Your letter touched me. It was from your heart, and I just started crying because it was a lot that I didn't even know. Please write to me again! I love you, Baby!

~

My mom sent me this text message on my birthday to top this story off with the perfect cherry.

"Hey, baby! I'm just up thinking about you! And I'm just so proud of you, baby! All that you've accomplished in your life at just the age of

21. Happy birthday, my baby! Mommy loves you so much, and I just wish you were here with me! You're strong, educated, wise, smart, gorgeous, and beautiful! And you want to know why? Because Beautiful Black Strong Women Matter! And I'm the proudest mother in the world! All because of Ms. Raven Ella Ozlyn! Happy 21st birthday, baby! I love you...we all love you...family and friends! You are an official adult."

Can you believe this made me cry tears of joy on my birthday? There was also the random Facebook post. It didn't make me cry, but it did boost my ego a bit.

"JUNE BABY"

You've got the best personality and are an absolute pleasure to be around. You love to make new friends and be outgoing. You are a great flirt, and more than likely have an attractive partner. A wicked hottie. It is more than likely. A hottie who has a massive record collection. You have a great choice in film and may one day become a famous actress yourself- heck, you've got the looks for it! In the next six days, you will meet someone that may become one of your closest friends if you repost this in five minutes."

I didn't repost it.

~

During the time I was at the hotel. I started talking to this guy, John Doe. He was sweet. I remember he texted me on Facebook. We started chatting. He was in the Army. Since I was stuck in the hotel for an extra week, I ended up spending my twenty-first birthday there. I didn't know anyone, and I had no friends, except for the few people I had met along the way. I did not know anyone well enough to ask for a favor.

Anyhow, he asked me, "What would you like for your birthday?" I responded, "Pepperoni Italian cheese bread from little Caesars and some cupcakes." It was a test. I didn't think he would do it. To my surprise, he did. He brought what I asked for to the hotel. It was so good too. I bought new movies that I had been dying to see from Amazon prime. I was living a good life that day. Even though I was trapped and couldn't leave, I made the most of it. The next day he brought me Popeye's – it was so delicious. They say the quickest way to a person's heart is through their stomach, I don't know if it was the inner phat girl in me talking or what.

~

We weren't officially together, though. After I moved on board, we decided that we would go on an actual date and go from there. Things were okay. It all went as planned.

I arrived on my ship Monday, June 22. That's the day I met OS2 Phillip. He was cool and he grabbed my bags for me. Then asked some basic questions on our way to the ship, like: How are you? How was the hotel? What do you like to do for fun? Where are you from? All the normal, basic stuff. We went to Hardee's before we went to the ship. I had never eaten there before. I ended up ordering a sandwich meal with some hash browns and a sweet tea. I never ate the sandwich because I was too nervous. I didn't know what to expect. Who was I going to see? How would this journey be? The only thing I knew for sure was that I was ready to get out of that hotel room.

We got to the pier and took a long walk to the ship. I didn't want to carry the body bag I had packed. OS2 did. When we passed the quarter-deck, he said, "fuck this shit, I'm tired." Then, he called some of the guys to help him. That's when I met Jerry and Richard. They were cool and carried my luggage to the female berthing for me. I just had to throw it in there, then go up top and join my division. I was in my dress whites. When I went upstairs, I was very quiet, just soaking in my new surroundings and new shipmates.

I was in the ops office when I saw him. I remember the wave of emotions when I first met him. He was handsome. In my mind, I'm thinking, "what's his name?" In a little while, everyone started introducing themselves to me. His name was Xavier. I remember thinking of playing it cool, just look and listen, so I did.

The environment was very playful. Everyone seemed comfortable with one another. Based on what just happened at A School, I wasn't fond of making any female friends. I was excited to know that there were only four women, including myself. One of whom would be leaving in a few weeks. The day went on and they eventually let me change from my dress whites into my in-dubs. Something way more comfortable.

June 30th, 2020

"You have power over your mind, not outside events. Realize this, and you will find strength."

~ Marcus Aurelius ~

Dear Diary,

It was the end of the workday, and everyone pretty much disbursed into their lives a little after 1300. I just stayed in the ops office for a while and then, it happened. I met Martha. She was on call for a vehicle inspection. She wasn't needed for the moment, so she came to the ops office to cool off. I was distant. I'm not fond of other women at first, something always ends up going wrong.

I remember her complaining. She had this high, squeaky voice. She just kept talking about how she didn't want to be outside in the heat. How she wanted some food, and she was tired. I was just looking at her engaging in conversation. She introduced herself to me and I did to her. I just was like I was going to keep an open mind. Eventually, I make my way to the berthing, and I meet YN1. She was a beautiful woman. She had dreads in her hair, was a bit loud and had a beautiful attitude.

She asked, "Do you want to go to Walmart and grab food?"

I said, "yes."

She made it very clear that she did not like that my division did not care for me about making sure I had soap, food, and necessities. I honestly hadn't realized it.

She said, "They should have made sure you were good."

I loved her personality and how she had my back from day one. I vowed to never burn that bridge. Fast forward: I finished out the work week. I was off the whole weekend because I wasn't put into a duty section yet. Of course, I spent the weekend with John Doe. We went on a date, and we talked about many things. We made the relationship official. He was nice and I liked him.

Over the next few weeks, I noticed things that I didn't like. He made comments that I was a lot darker than his normal type. He said he would usually go for lighter-skinned girls. I'm thinking, "okay and look what that light skin did to you. She got pregnant while she was still your girlfriend. Then, dared to try and make you take care of it." So that was strike one. Strike two was when he ignored my family who came down to see me for the Fourth of July.

The weekend was pretty awesome. I got to spend it with my family. It would be my first time seeing them in seven months. They couldn't come to my graduation because of the COVID-19 outbreak. I was beyond excited to see them.

~ R.E.O. ~

July 12th, 2020

"The reason why we can't let go of someone is that deep inside, we still have hope."

~ Anonymous ~

Dear Diary,

Today I went to the Nex. I got a ride there from an ensign from another ship. It worked out. I thank the Lord I was allowed to get there and back safely. I pray the Lord continues to bless my friends and family. I like Xavier, and I found out he likes me back, but I can't pursue him. I got a good thing going on with John. I am not going to do anything to mess it up. I created my five-year plan today.

~ R.E.O. ~

~~~~~~

I know we had just started dating. However, my family could come on base, but I wouldn't set them up for failure. In terms of well I know my family. On the base are regular police and base police. So, I asked John to pick me up last night and bring me back to the ship. He said, okay. The thing was, they were going to see me leave with a stranger, so I asked him to introduce himself. He said he didn't want to do it. He just wanted to stay in the car. My family walked me to the car, so he had no choice but to say hi. That was a red flag. We continued to see each other every weekend. He dropped me back off at my ship on Sunday nights.

Strike number three was when he explained that he wasn't currently working. He just checked in through a call or text with whomever oversees him. He said he pretended to be suicidal for his disability percentage to go up. He has a genetic problem with his spine, so even when he gets out of the Army, they would pay him a paycheck for the rest of his life. He had a percentage of 20%, then he pretended to be crazy and brought it up to 40%. I was completely taken aback. I'm like, what the hell! Who would have the courage and the determination to do that crazy shit?

So I asked, "how were the thirty days in the psych ward? Like, what did you do?" He said, "every day, they asked how he was feeling and what he wanted to do?" He would respond, "not so much suicidal today." Or "today might be my last day." I was shaking. I called my Nana and told her about that crazy conversation. She said, "that's not normal." Plus, it showed a lot about his character. He didn't want to work. He just wanted to live off the government for the rest of his life. In addition, to having an active-duty title.

I did continue to see him. It wouldn't be long before things came to an end, though. Strike number four was when we went to Walmart. The lady who rang us up noticed that we paid for our things separately. He also didn't offer to carry my bags. She leaned over and said to me, "a man that does not support, is not a man at all." She did not like him very much. He reached for my bags and tried to hurry up and leave, so, we did. We went back to his place. He was talking, and I told him I was interested in someone else. He looked at me, and I said, "Well, this person is interested in me too." He was like, "how do you know?" "Because someone told me," I replied.

By the next night, I find myself text-dumped and to top things off, completely blocked. I was shocked, like I did not know where this came from. I can laugh about it now. In the heat of the moment, I asked myself, "Am I sad?" The answer was no. I just wished he hadn't blocked me on everything so I could have responded. I also left a few things at his place. He kicked my ass to the curb so fast, honestly, I wasn't sad. I just thought, "well, that puts me back on the market for Xavier."

Chapter 3 Part 1: By No Means, A Sister's Keeper

Dear Diary,

I got over John Doe quickly. I was just going to work and live peacefully on the ship. I didn't have a car, so I was just stuck. Again, I didn't care, and I made the most of it. I'm independent. I caught rides to the store. I even attempted to walk a couple of times. I love spending time by myself. I am beyond comfortable being alone. The only thing was Martha was also stuck. After the first couple of weeks of me staying on board, this is what happened.

To commence, Martha was so happy and excited that she was engaged to a guy named Jawan. He joined a different branch. He was at A School hanging out with this girl and they were being extra friendly. Long story short, the female was way friendlier than all his other friends. On this day, Jawan wants to break things off with Martha. Martha and I had only been cordial up to this point. After receiving the text messages, she throws her phone across the room in the lounge. She starts crying and getting upset. They broke up through text messages, he was leaving her for the girl.

I didn't know how to comfort her. Then again, I don't like seeing people upset. So, I go over pat and rub her shoulder, trying to comfort her. And so, I ask her, "What's wrong?" It took a little minute, but she started painting the picture for me. At the time, I was on her side. I said, "it was wrong for him to do that to you. He should have been honest from the beginning. He may have intended to be honest and forthcoming; only he and God know."

At the same time, both joined two different branches. They weren't stationed in the same area. The odds were endless. Of course, I'm telling her not to cry and that everything is going to be all right. I'm just letting her vent her frustrations. I remember she called her friend and discussed everything. I just went back to my phone and back on YouTube. When she wanted to cry and talk about it again, I was there for her. Honestly, I felt terrible, and I shared the recent events that I went through. I wasn't sad, though. We just joked it off. That's the day we started to bond.

Our friendship continued. We both arrived at the same time. So of course, they always paired us up together. I love work. I hate being late. I love to eat breakfast. So, I'm always on my shit. Waking up and going upstairs to join my division, that was no problem. Being respectful to everyone, no problem either. Martha was a different breed. Almost every day, I needed to grab Martha from her rack to go to work, join the division, or convince her to work on a qual or something. I was brand new.

On the other hand, Martha is always complaining. Always says she's tired. Very rude. Very entitled. Always playing. She never knew the difference between a time to play and a time to be serious. All these things, they were what everybody pointed out. I kept hearing the same comments. She is flat-out annoying and aggravating. She's loud and doesn't want to do anything. I noticed those things too. Ironically, at the same time, everyone kept pushing her on me. Nobody wanted to be responsible for her. I don't mind helping others, but at the same time, I am not a babysitter. Being Martha's "friend" is exactly what it felt like being a babysitter.

"Make sure you and Martha get your qualifications together!" "Make sure Martha is up for the underway!" "Where is Martha?" "Go get her from her rack!" At first, I thought, I understand, we are the only two females besides the other two who are higher-ups. They just expected too much from me. I did play the role for about ninety days, then I had to cut her off. I couldn't be her friend anymore. Let me rewind and tell you the full story.

I explained that Martha's boyfriend called it quits with her. She was never focused on work. She was more boy crazy. It was that weekend when she started talking about Tom. He was one of our shipmates. He was buff and tan. He would have been considered a dream guy if you were interested. He happened to have a duty that weekend, so she made her move.

Tom and Martha met up and later that night Martha and I talked about the situation, we were cool. I just always stay to myself. I didn't consider her my friend yet. Anyway, she comes back and she's like, "Tom and I snuck into marine berthing. We talked for a bit and he gave her an innocent kiss on the cheek." Of course, venting to me, she kept talking about how she wanted a kiss on the lips but he was too much of a gentleman.

I responded, "he seems sweet and nice. I'm glad you're not upset. I'm glad you're moving on." The very next time they were leaving the same berthing, people were walking up to the location where they were. Tom told her to go in the opposite direction. Martha responded, "Not without a kiss". He kissed her on the cheek and she was upset. He then proceeded to kiss her on the lips.

That was the weekend, so now it is the following week. A few days later, someone mentions that Tom has a girlfriend. Martha was upset again. I'm pretty sure she asked him about it through text message. He said, "Yes, he did or something along the lines of it's complicated." Then, he told her that he just wanted to be friends.

Later, when it was asked why did Tom stop talking to Martha? He answered, "I sensed she was trouble." If only he could have known how 100% correct, he was? I wish I had known.

That weekend Martha thinks of a plan to get with Jerry. She says at a get-together with the other OS, apparently, he was feeling up her leg while he was drunk. In her conclusion, she thought it would be a good idea to hook up with him. Her exact words were, "I just want someone to beat my back in." She had to hatch up a plan to get off base so he could go and pick her up.

Jerry was our leading petty officer (LPO) at the time. Of course, they didn't want to be seen together. She kept asking me what I thought or how did I feel about any of it? I just kept saying, well, if that's what you want to do. I would not have done what she was doing. At the end of the conversation, she will make her own decision. Which she did.

She went over to one of the female OS' apartments that weekend. Jerry picked her up, and they hooked up. The next day of course, the question was, was it worth it? She said, "no, the sex was terrible."

Moving forward going into the week, Xavier put it out there that he liked me. I said, "I like him too." I remember I liked him a lot. I never really talked to him, though. I do recall meeting Max and having conversations with him. It was the "where are you from" question when we met. I'm from Florida is what Max told me. My exact words were, "oh, you're from Florida? I know you are trifling. All the men that I know from Florida are." I didn't know at the time what his angle was.

I remember thinking he wasn't any good. I just didn't know his exact motives yet. I do remember everyone kept bringing up a girl named Heather. They kept suggesting that he got her pregnant and he kept denying it. Someone mentioned that he had met her father. They kept asking the question, "What happened when you met Heather's father?" Max's story was that he and Heather were terrific friends. He said he happened to be at the same gas station as Heather when she decided to introduce him to her father. He said they both greeted each other and that was the end of it. Now I'm not 'Booboo the fool' as they say, so I know there was a hell of a lot more to that story. I was brand new to the ship when this was in the air so to me, I didn't really care.

Anyway, we would all go buy lunch during the week. A couple of people would do a run for everybody. You just had to send the money to pay for your food, of course. I remember Max being extra nice. He bought my

Panda Express. Just like I said, I knew he was no good, I just hadn't completely figured him out yet.

I believe it was Wednesday when I had to go run a task with Xavier. It was the both of us together working on something. He mentions that he heard I liked him. I responded, "Yes, I do." He says, "Well if you want to talk, we can talk." I said, "We'll talk later." Everyone was going to Buffalo Wild Wings later to watch some basketball game. He was going to be there, so, I said, "we can have a conversation later." Fast forward, it was the end of the workday. We all go home and freshen up to meet up later.

A shipmate named Stanley had just bought his car. He was willing to pick everyone up and drive to the restaurant. It's Stanley, Martha, and I loaded up into the car to pick up Max. Xavier had his own car, so he agreed to meet us at the restaurant. The whole time I'm in the car, I'm texting Xavier and having an entire conversation. Next thing I know, Stanley mentions that Xavier is bringing his girlfriend. My heart sinks. My brain had a panic attack full of thoughts. I'm already in the car on my way to the restaurant, now I feel this rush of emotions.

I can't leave, I don't have a car. We are already out and about. Mind you, this is my first time going out into the city. I texted Xavier, "do you have a girlfriend?" He paused and texted back, "yes." I was so upset that I wanted to cry. I thought, "Why would he do that to me?" I also remember thinking, "no, I have to see this for myself." We get to the restaurant, and he is sitting at the table with his girlfriend. I was so shocked. I remember moving in to get a closer look. After the group sat down, they asked if we all wanted something to drink. I don't even think it was two minutes later and my tears came rushing down. I rushed to the restroom and thankfully, Martha followed me. My heart was pounding. I went into the stall and tears were streaming down my face like a river. I felt so embarrassed. It felt like everyone was staring at me; it made me feel so stupid. I had no idea why he would do that to me. All I knew was that I had to get out of there. When I turned around from wiping my eyes, all I see is Martha on the phone.

I remember that brief thought of "what the fuck?" I'm going through a crisis and you're going to take a fucking phone call. I just reached into my back pocket for my phone. Trying to call someone. Anyone. I honestly didn't care who. I just really needed to get the fuck out of that restaurant.

Then, I decided to call one of the other OS females, Sarah. When I called, she tried to give me an excuse about how she couldn't. I just kept mentioning it was an emergency. I know she didn't want to invite me over.

Later, I would learn the real reason why. It had nothing to do with me, of course. When I found out, I clearly understood the reason.

Anyway, she eventually starts asking me, "are you crying? What's wrong?" And I said, "I will tell you once I'm with you. As for right now, I just need to leave." She sends me her address, and I'm about to step outside to take an Uber or a Lyft to her place. Martha happens to finish her phone call. Now she's concerned and she's asking me, "What are you going to do?" My only answer is, "I'm leaving, I'm going to Sarah's house."

There is no way I can go back to that table and watch him sit there with his hand around another girl. Let alone right in front of his girlfriend. Martha did offer to leave with me. In her eyes, you could tell that she didn't want to leave even if I really had wanted her to. She would have complained the entire time, as she always does.

So I told her, "No, you go. Go have a good time. I'm going to make my way back to the ship." When I think back on this situation. If the roles were reversed, because eventually they would be there was no way I would have stayed and had drinks with those people. I would have up and left if I was a true friend. Little did I know, Martha was not my friend, and she never was.

After I arrived at Sarah's house, we talked and discussed all the details about what happened. I really should have listened to her advice. I guess I just had to see it all for myself.

Sarah said something along the lines of Xavier is like a dog. He is not a bad person; he just sniffs around looking for a bone. She said he was not someone I should waste my time with. Sarah also told me that I should just keep a professional relationship with Martha and try not to be a buddy. She stated she knows it's hard because they always pair us up together, but I should keep my distance.

She said when Max first came on board, he was interested in getting things done. Now, he was super lazy and wanted everything handed to him. Sarah was spot on. She read those people better than I did. I can read people very well but sometimes it takes time.

I believe it all has to do with that first impression. They all gave me a great first impression. Sarah's first impression was that she didn't want to be bothered with me. She had her reasons too. It was all because of Martha.

When Martha first came to the ship. Sarah opened her house and home for her. Only for Martha to be entitled, rude and disrespectful towards her. She had burned a bridge. Two weeks later, I would need to get to the other side. It only takes one person to ruin it for everyone else. That's why when I came, no one offered to help me out. They had been so lovely to Martha just for her to spit in their faces. They were not keen on doing it again. It completely sucked, but it made sense.

I ended up spending that night with Sarah. She had a couple of errands to run. We talked and went to the store together. I grabbed some Taco Bell, and she grabbed sushi. We went back to her place and watched some tv. I slept on her couch while she went to her bed. I cried myself to sleep that night. I kept telling Sarah and myself that I had learned my lesson. I was so headstrong and utterly convinced that I was done. Little did I know there was a plan the devil was hatching up.

I went back to the ship with Sarah the next day to go to work. I was okay and no longer upset. I just wanted to be back in my comfort zone. When I went to join my division, Xavier was sitting on the floor looking like a sad puppy. In my head, I'm thinking, "why is he sad?" I should be the one upset. Max asked Martha why I left, and she told him. Max confronted Xavier about the stunt that he pulled at the restaurant. When I tell you I booked it, I did not go back to the table for anything.

I remember when Max confronted me and told me he had no idea what was going on. He told me, If he had known, he would have handled it. I responded, "It's okay, I'm okay. I learned my lesson. I won't be climbing up that tree anymore."

Later that day, I ran into Xavier when I was coming from the laundry room. He was apologizing to me and trying to explain. He said, "He did not know I liked him like that." A whole lie. I said," yeah, I did. But I learned my lesson. You're good. Don't worry." This is my red flag. I always do this. It's like basic emotions. This makes me angry, sad, happy, whatever the case. I'm just so independent I don't want anybody to be the reason behind my emotional well-being.

I just expect to be disappointed by people. That's why I just expect the worst. I keep saying things are okay, and they are not. What he did was not okay, and it was never okay. If I could have had a chance to redo that conversation, would have given it to him straight. I did not deserve to be treated like that. I should have embarrassed him at that restaurant as he did to me.

By the same token, I know myself, and I am not confrontational. I would rather walk away. That is what I did, I walked away. Now I have so much anxiety going to Buffalo Wild Wings. I hate that restaurant with a passion.

A couple of days later, Martha was gossiping about what happened at Buffalo Wild Wings. How Max was coming on to her. I'm pretty sure I was in my own world when I had a conversation with myself. I said, "I learned my lesson about Xavier. I will stay clear." The next thing I know, Martha wants me to go for a walk with her and Max on base.

I said, "If he is coming on to you, why does he want me to go?"

She's like, "he doesn't want you to go for a walk." She said, "I just invited you because I don't want to be seen alone with him." That's why she wanted me to tag along. I knew the red flag. I felt like a third wheel. It was awkward. I tried to make the most of it. It ended up being an enjoyable night. We asked so many personal questions and got to know each other better. We ended up being there and talking until like 2 or 3 am.

The only major problem about that night was when the question came up about what was your worst sexual experience? Everybody gave their answer. However, Martha decided to reference the hookup she had with Jerry. Of course, if she had said his name, we would have known who she was talking about. So, she referenced him as J boy. Long story short, she vented about how he was terrible in bed. The red flag was when she said, "Being with him was like rape."

Once she made that statement, I immediately confronted her about that. I said, "Wait, no. You cannot say that." Max was also saying something along the lines of you wouldn't know that." I wish I didn't have to bring race into this situation. Martha is mixed or Native American. If you ask me, she is confused.

Anyway, when she first got to the ship, she hung out with Hispanic or white people. When I got there, I leaned more towards black people. It has been scientifically proven that people like to venture toward people like them. Martha, just as I said, is confused. She doesn't know whether she wants to be white or black. I only mention this because Jerry, Max, Xavier, and I are black. For her to say anything along the lines of rape is disgusting.

Martha initiated everything. She texted him and decided how they would get together. She even told me that she had made her way to his bed and waited for him to join her. Her exact words were, "I want to feel something. I want someone to break my back in." The point of the story is, she consented to everything. Just because Martha was trying to get Max, doesn't make it okay for her to throw around lies about Jerry.

If anyone heard that, she felt forced into having sex with him, she could have ruined his career. What would make her think making that comment was ever okay? Once Max and I confronted her about it. She recanted and said it wasn't, however; that major incident made me look at her differently.

I knew from that conversation a lot about her character and logic, that she is also a big liar. She will say anything to make herself look better. We all continued to chat and have a good time. I took a mental note about that red flag because that made me completely angry.

The following day, Martha, Max, Xavier, and I are all stuck on the ship. They told Xavier how we all bonded and how he should have been there. That night they wanted to play truth or dare. I said well, you guys have fun. They wanted me to tag along, and I said, "No, he has a girlfriend; why would I play this game?" Peer pressure, I guess. I would have been a party pooper, is the term.

Martha said, "It's just a game; don't take it seriously. Come play." She didn't want to play the game with both the guys by herself. Eventually, I agreed to play. It was fun and funny. I had a great time. I. guess Xavier did too because he invited me over to his barracks at the end of the game. I was surprised he asked me. I said, "Yes." After all, I did like him.

I kept telling myself maybe I could forgive him for "the incident". Perhaps I could put this behind me. My head knew better, but my emotions were in the business of making bad decisions. The next day after work had been a long one. He went home and straightened up, I guess. Martha just wanted some Panda Express. She started complaining that she didn't want to walk to his car to grab the food. She was hot and upset. I overlooked her because I was excited to hang out with him. I got in his car and went back to his barracks. I ate my Panda Express at his place.

We talked and bonded. There was a lot of eye contact. I let down my guard, and I have no idea why. I did want to get to know him and as a result, we had a great night. We hooked up, I was definitely upset with myself. I don't deserve to be anybody's second choice or backup plan. I can't believe I let myself fall into that predicament.

Later, down the line. I asked him to choose between his girlfriend and me. He picked her...twice. Even though he was spending all his time with me.

He wanted me to tag along with him everywhere. I was the one he was cuddled up with at night, I accepted the way he was. When I found out the background between him and his girlfriend, I said, "what the fuck?"

They met, they exchanged numbers, she ghosted him for two entire months. Then, they happened to run into each other again. He was with her for two weeks before he met me for the first time on the ship. He found out I had a boyfriend and that's why he didn't reach out to me or anything. We had chemistry from the first time we saw one another. I knew I wasn't the only one that felt it.

Anyway, Xavier and I both wanted something. I know I wanted to be with him, and I think he wanted the same thing. He was just being a follower. Max wanted to be with Martha, but he had his own chick on the side. Max gave off the impression that Xavier was his best friend. When I found out later that their friendship was like mine and Martha's. I was just speechless.

Days go by and we are all hanging out with one another. Then, it's Max and Xavier's duty day. Martha knows how to drive, and I don't, so she suggests that I ask Xavier for his car to go to the mall. I said, "Okay. I'll ask." And well, I asked. Of course, he says yes to me. We went to the mall and had a great time. We ate at Charlie's, it was delicious. We end up being out all day and bringing some food back for the guys.

The only problem we ran into was not remembering how to get back on base. The exit we used was now closed, so we had to use a different gate. There was a Walgreens or a McDonald's right next to the closed gate. I told Martha to go there for a second while I reach out and ask for directions. She doesn't listen. She goes behind the Walgreens or McDonald's into a sketchy area. Then, she stops in front of a weird house and apartment. I said, "Just turn around." Martha says, "No, I'm going to cut through this street in front of us that says one way." I said, "no, because it says one way." She goes down the street anyway instead of going the way we came. She hits a pothole.

I'm upset because I'm telling her exactly what to do, and she is not comprehending the common sense that I'm telling her. She is just so anxious to be driving it's like her common sense is out the window. She hits the pothole and goes down the one-way street, ending up back at Walgreens or McDonald's. We sit there for a minute in the parking lot finally reaching out to somebody on the ship to get directions back to base.

As we are driving, she hears a noise and asks me do I hear it? After I stopped and listened, I said, "Yeah, I do." We pull over and look underneath the car. Xavier's cover is dragging underneath the car. We both panicked. I promised nothing was going to happen to his car. I told him he could trust Martha. Martha says, "He's going to be so mad at me. "I'm saying, "It's okay. We are going to figure everything out." Then, out of nowhere, Martha says, "Can you tell Xavier that you messed up his car and hit a pothole?" I say, "No, I wasn't the one driving, and why would you suggest that?" She says, "Xavier likes you. He's not going to get mad if you say it was you."

Red flag, I already know. That made me upset. Why would she even suggest that as an option? If it was something serious, she would have no problem throwing me under the bus. Wow! What a great friend? Then, Martha says we should not tell Xavier what happened to his car to make matters worse. I said, "That is not an option either. We are going to tell him what happened to his car." She calls Max, and he says, "I wouldn't tell him what happened; I would just give him back the car and let him say something to you guys about it."

I respond, "No, we tell Xavier what happened to his car. That is the only logical thing to do because if somebody borrowed your car and something happened to it, you would want to know." I think this was when I started to take mental notes about Martha and Max. This would be the second red flag.

~

August 1st, 2020

Dear Diary,

What one-worded words would I use to describe myself?

I (Raven Ella Ozlyn) am so many words that the list is infinite. There is no way I can jot down one word being that in the end, I am a lovely prize. As I am entering this month of August, I realize a lot of things. I spent all yesterday with Xavier. We are on the same page now, probably because I got a lot off my chest, and he did as well. We enjoyed ourselves in each other's company. But it's time that I move on. I got a find someone who is no question going to make me they're number one. I'm going to leave him alone. I'm going to date someone else. See what other fishes are in the sea.

I know he's not the one. But who says I can't have a little fun? Xavier is going to realize I'm the one when it's too late. Xavier and I are just not meant to be. I need to cut him off and grow by myself. And I will continue to focus on myself.

I am also worried about seeing my family. I love them. My dad is my dad, and I can't exchange him. Spent the night in my room. I am excited to spend time with my family. I love my life. I love the person I am. I love the God that's my Heavenly Father, and he's giving me the right directions. I pray that you keep everything in my best interest. I am excited. I do want to see everyone. I love them. I know my blessing is coming. My family is all a bunch of roller coasters.

~ R.E.O. ~

September 2nd, 2020

Dear Diary,

Today I got OC spray. It went a lot better than I expected. I got the video and posted it for everyone to see. I am not sure if I logged what happened on Saturday or not, but Sunday was perfect. I spent it with Xavier and it was terrific. We enjoyed each other 's company. The whole time I thought about many things between him and me. Why he's so suitable for me? I guess because we don't make sense. Since we don't make sense, I think we make sense. I just realized that I might be falling for him. Number 44 on how to love is loving them even if they are temporarily unavailable to give you love in return.   ~ R.E.O. ~

After all the surf bravo training, we did for the past 3 weeks, this is the day we had to get OC sprayed to pass the class. They just pepper spray us because you can't use it on other people and do not know how it feels. That is not the reason; that is just my opinion. The real reason is that if you OC spray somebody and accidentally spray yourself, you must be able to fight through it.

I was nervous because I don't eat spicy foods. I'm thinking, what if I react terribly? Everybody was pumped for it. Me, Martha, Stanley, and Parker. We all decided to record the sprays on my phone because I had an iPhone 11 Pro. I had three cameras, and it was the most updated phone. I didn't mind. I'm not sure about the order we went in. Stanley got sprayed, and he did well. He got punched and kicked around a bit. As well as Parker.

Martha decided she wanted to go first, and then I would go next. She gets OC sprayed, and she makes a complete fool of herself. She overreacted a million percent. It was hilarious. Watching it in real life, her outburst left the whole crowd speechless. I don't like to be embarrassed. In my mind, I'm thinking, no matter how much this hurts, I promised not to react like her.

Martha makes it through the course, and she made it out alive. I get OC sprayed. I did not blink right away; I thought I could squint my way through. When it came time to hit the target as it was moving. I had to open my eyes to that. The MAC at the time says, "Open your eyes!" I say, "I can't!" He yells back, "yes, you can! Don't ever say you can't!" Or something similar. So, I start to blink. Come to find out, it wasn't that bad. It didn't even hurt after the first minute. I got through the course. The red man kicked me, and I fell. Other than that, I got through it like a champ.

Fifteen minutes later, my eyes were magnificent. I washed them out with the baby soap I brought for everyone to use. I was sitting there on Facebook watching the other people. It was so hilarious to me. They were dying, figuratively speaking, like Martha and many other people.

If I had to get OC sprayed again, I would. It was so much fun. I had duty, so I took a nap. Not in my rack, of course. I did not want the residue to get on my pillow or blanket. I was on the ship while Martha went to the barracks with the guys. Later, I took a shower when I got up from my nap. I had no re-flash or anything. That was a day I was proud of. A job well done!

~ R.E.O. ~

September 3rd, 2020

Dear Diary,

It is extremely hot, for real. OC sprayed yesterday. My eyes are perfectly fine. I miss Xavier. I like him. When he touches me, I just know I got to have him. I don't want to sound crazy. I need to give it time and more experience. Only time will tell.

It is so hot in the living space. Tonight, we are sleeping in our workspace. Martha went down for cranking. When she comes back, it's my turn. I wish we could stay together. Xavier is leaving for another department, maybe. I'm going to miss him if that happens. I know we are still going to see each other. Xavier has been the main topic a lot. I swear he is always in my heart. My stomach is super upset. I ate some smothered fish from the mess decks. Now my tummy is super messed up. Right now, my leave starts Monday after 1600 and my flight leaves around 1800, so I'm good.

~ R.E.O. ~

September 4th, 2020

Dear Diary,

We hung out and had a great night back at the barracks. Xavier, Max, Martha, and I. We had alcohol, we danced, played music, joked, and played games. We just had a great time. We had white liquor. Max was the main supplier. We hung out the whole weekend.

~ R.E.O. ~

September 5th, 2020

Dear Diary,

I remember this day because it was crazy. We partied late last night, but I had a hair appointment set for the morning. I went to this hair salon called Shear's Lounge. I love this place, it's a 10 out of 10. I spend so much money here. Later, I knew we would be going to one of our shipmates' birthday celebrations at his house. He was a cool dude. I looked great and we went to this party later. Our other friend thought I said, "I can drink or do something silly." When what I really said was, "I never drank/pre-gamed before." He thought I was challenging him. Why after the sixth shot, I was going down?

I walked into the party, then Xavier walked me outside. As soon as we hit the streets, I threw up. Disgusting, I know. I said, "that's not cute at all." He said, "That's okay, it's normal." He put me in the car. We went to another party, and I was in the car the whole time. My stomach was agitated. I'm pretty sure it was because I was drinking dark liquor and the night before, but I usually drink white liquor. I was suffering.

~ R.E.O. ~

September 8th, 2020

Dear Diary,

The Seven Rules of Life

1) Let it go. Never ruin a good day by thinking about a bad yesterday.

2) Ignore them. Don't listen to other people. Live a life that's empowering to you.

3) Give it time. Time heals everything.

4) Don't compare. The only person you should try to beat is the person you were yesterday.

5) Stay calm. It's okay to not have everything figured out. Know that in times, you'll get there.

6) It's on you. Only you are in control of your happiness.

7) Smile! Life is short; enjoy it while you have it.

I went back home to Miami. In the beginning, I couldn't go to Miami because of COVID-19. Then, Florida became a red state. Max was allowed to go to Florida because it became a green state. Long story short, I wanted to go back home and check on my family. They needed me. My dad is something else. I caught a flight to Miami. Let me tell you, my stomach was so upset, I had Pepto Bismol as my soft drink flying back home. I had to play it cool, but I was dying underneath that mask. I made it back home safe and sound.

~ R.E.O. ~

September 9th, 2020

"Nobody is more stubborn than an android person that won't switch to iPhone."

~ Internet joke ~

Dear Diary,

This reminded me of Xavier. I enjoyed the time I spent back home. I had relax with my family and rejoiced with my family and little sister.

September 14th, 2020

Dear Diary,

I was headed back to Virginia. I love my family, but I like being out and about. No tabs and living life. So it was time for me to go back to my new home, Virginia. While back home in Florida, Xavier and his girlfriend broke up. I was excited because I knew he deserved so much better than her. She didn't care about him from how she treated him. This is also the first time I let down my guard to cope with what I wanted. I was wrong. I should have backed off completely. The truth is I didn't. I was interested and so was he.

~ R.E.O. ~

September 21st, 2020

Dear Diary,

Last time I wrote in my diary I was at Xavier's place. Just having a conversation with him sends me to the moon. This past week with him, exploring each other's minds and enjoying each other's company has been more than impressive. He makes me feel so amazing. I don't want anything to go wrong. I never felt this way with anyone. I'm trying to protect my feelings, but they are so strong for him. I have no idea why I trust him 100%. I can have a future with him. He mentioned love first. He is the one I want. He is the man I'm looking for. I just don't want this to be one-sided.

~ R.E.O. ~

September 26th, 2020

Dear Diary,

I know which officer program I want to join. I am doing well, but at the same time, I feel alone. I met this great guy who could be the one. He got all these insecurities. And we are connecting and spending a lot of time together. Like, every waking moment. But he is asking me to give him time. I know that's what he needs, and I know that is what's needed. It's just, I don't need time. I know I will give everything to God and let things work out. I gave him my love card. I told my Nana about Martha, and she thinks she is toxic and not worth my friendship. She's probably right. It's because of how she is. I talk to her because lately, she has been making me angry. I love my family. I love my home. I know my life is slowly coming together.

Martha suggested I should go see someone else and I said, "No, I can't because Xavier and I are working on things." I asked her "would she leave Max alone?" Then she said, "she wouldn't distance herself from Max". She wouldn't distance herself from Max, but why would she be suggesting that I distance myself from Xavier? I realize that Martha is prejudiced, and I see it just by her saying the N-word. I know I'm not in competition with her because I know who I am. It's like she's got to be the center of attention, and everything must revolve around her. I'm going to have to slowly distance myself from Martha.

~ R.E.O. ~

September 29th, 2020

Dear Diary,

I find myself going through the same dilemma. Honestly, I'm going to have to stop being friends with Martha. I'm drained. Max is on the fence as well. I am going to Destin to distance myself and not say anything.

So today, I am going to stop being friends with Martha. I am primarily giving her tough love, but I can also give myself peace of mind. I am so tired. I need to distance myself. She needs to think for herself and so do I. If I am in trouble or anything, I would at least like it to be because of something I did. I feel this is precisely what is needed. I don't trust Max. Just thinking about how he dogged Xavier and the man who let him use his car for a month. I cannot get over everything. I asked Xavier to do a driving lesson today. But I'm not feeling up for it.

~ R.E.O. ~

September 30th, 2020

Dear Diary,

Not being friends with Martha has brought me some peace of mind. We are supposed to talk today. I'm up for it, especially since Xavier is acting like he's upset with me about the situation. I know he and Max are claiming they have the exact situation, but the difference is, I don't babysit them. We are not y'all. And people just keep trying to give her an excuse. I am not a babysitter. I can't keep doing that.

In your opinion, what is the most toxic personality trait?

In my opinion, the most toxic trait would be a very entitled person. Thinking that everyone and the world owes you something, I dislike a person who thinks everything is supposed to be handed to them. I work for everything I have. That feels good to say; yeah, I did this for me. I've realized that Xavier, he is my little boo thang. Lord knows we are both getting comfortable with each other. But I don't have to deal with Martha.

~ R.E.O. ~

Around this time, my friend Fred had finally made it to the ship. He was very vocal about how he wanted to go out and about to hang out. Stanley and Fred hung out together a lot. Stanley was married and had a wife. He was able to get an apartment for himself and his family. Until his wife came into town, he allowed Fred to come over. Makes sense because they are boys, I guess.

Once Stanley's wife came into town, Fred became a big baby in a sense. He was mopey and kept saying things like, "Oh, since Stanley's wife came, he doesn't invite me over no more." "I wish I had somewhere to hang." "Where y'all be going? What y'all be doing?" "I want to come." Point number one, Stanley had already told Fred that he had to bounce as soon as his wife came. Why was he acting like this was news to him? I do not understand. If Stanley had made any other plans to accommodate his wife, I am pretty sure he and Fred could be stuck at the ship together.

Fred kept insinuating to me that he wanted to tag along. I kept telling him that it was not my car. How am I supposed to invite somebody else as a guest when I am a guest myself? I told him he had to ask Xavier because that was his car. He wanted to go and hang out with Richard.

On this day we all went to Richard's house. Xavier, Max, Martha, Fred, and me, we all had a great time. We went to PF Chang's and met up with Parker, his wife Deborah and Richard and his wife, Kayla. After that, we all went to Richard and Kayla's place, except for Parker and Deborah; they had kids to tend to. Before we left the restaurant, Xavier was going to buy my food. Max was going to pay for his and Martha's food. Out of thin air, Fred decided to pay the whole tab for everyone. He said something along the lines of, "the navy isn't my only income. I do this kind of stuff." Then, he ended it all sentimental by saying, "he appreciated Xavier bringing him along; he appreciated being invited out. If we've got his back. He's got ours." I thought it was weird, and he only did it to fit in. Fred tends to act differently around different people. You should never have to buy anyone's friendship.

Fast forward a bit, we get to Richard's place. We meet the dog, blast music, and start passing out drinks. Then, people started pulling out their dance moves. Xavier was a great dancer. His go-to song is *The Party* by Chris Brown. I used to love it when he danced. Fred danced to some New Jersey music. He did a great job. It was all entertaining. We all laughed and joked. I believe we all went for a walk and Xavier carried me on his neck. He is so silly at times. He said he had to pee, so he found a tree and went from there. Now that I'm thinking about it. He did not wash his hands. Just nasty. We went back to Richard's place and blasted music until 1 in the morning. Kayla tried to tell us in the most excellent way that "you ain't got to go home, but you got to get the fuck out of here." I love Kayla. She is amazing.

This is the week where things went south with Martha and me. I had already noticed toxicity in her and the reputation that surrounded her. She just does not have any respect for anybody. She has no manners and does not have a filter. She is entitled and acts like everything is about her, she complains all the time, she does not want to work. She does not have a sense of when it's time to work or play. She just wants to be boy crazy. She doesn't want to work for anything, and she takes no responsibility; nor is she accountable for her actions. She is a big liar and a cheater; she also has no morals or ethics. All these things were reflected in her shitty friendship.

I called my auntie, and we had a long discussion about the incidents that led me to my conclusion. For example, Martha went cranking a few weeks prior and she complained the whole time. She did not care that we headed back to the barracks around 1400. If she got off work at 1900 she expected and wanted Xavier to go pick her up from the ship. In addition to her having to be back on the ship at four in the morning, she expected Xavier to also be okay with dropping her off when the rest of us had to be to work at 0700. She was just unbelievable. The nerve of her.

Whenever Max said jump, she didn't ask how high, she just did it. For example, I know Xavier had a girlfriend. She kept telling me don't take it too seriously. I said, "Yea. I got that." At the same time, she was moving in with Max at his barracks. She carried a lot of her shit over there. Whenever they got into a disagreement, he would be quick to pack up all her shit and put it by the front door. He did it twice before I tried to give her some advice.

I told her you never give a man the opportunity to kick you out, you get your own space. You have your own back. Do not allow this man to be able to tell you to leave. I would never move in with my boyfriend. Maybe that is just a personal preference, but I am not moving in if you are not my husband. I told her I was still working on getting my barracks. I would leave some things here and there, but as far as thinking this is your place of residence as well, nah. That ain't the move. I said she was listening, but I talked to a damned wall.

Another thing is Max went out with friends, he said some of his friends were women. In summary, he did not invite Martha. She cried the whole time he was gone. She wanted to drive Xavier's car around the base all night until he came back. Xavier and I wanted to go to sleep. Me being the good friend that I am, I went outside to support and comfort her in her time of need. Did she do the same for me at the restaurant? *Fuck, no!* That was in the back of my mind. After we drove around for an hour, I told her, "I'm gonna go to sleep. I'm tired." She did all that for nothing. Xavier says, "I don't want her to run my battery out. I don't want to go to sleep with her driving around late by herself." I thought she was being overdramatic and acting desperate. Y'all have been talking for a week, and you act like this. You need to get it together. I went and told her what he said. At midnight, I indeed went to bed. Later that night, Max came back and she was excellent, perfectly fine.

Let me clarify that we had all been partying at Richard's place on Sunday night. That Thursday, we would be going on an underway that was roughly a month long. Monday morning came around and Max texted our chief his auntie has COVID. Even if his auntie did have COVID, how did that affect him? He was nowhere near his auntie the whole weekend. He claims that he was around his auntie who tested positive for COVID. They did not allow Max to come on board the ship.

October 5th, 2020

Dear Diary,

I already knew that everyone was begging me to make friends with Martha, but it's something about Max. I mean, I'm gonna let go of all of my concerns. I'm going to let the martyr learn her lesson the hard way. I cannot stress enough, but this weekend was great. I enjoyed it. We spent it at our friend's house and Xavier and I were getting close. Which is fine with me. I called my family to let them in on everything. They are doing great and so am I.

~ R.E.O. ~

When I spoke to my auntie and told her about the deal with Martha. She told me, "Don't tell her anything. If she wants to be stupid for Max, let her be stupid for Max. Just do your job and stay out of it. Because she is going to do what she wants to do. "That's what I kept in mind strictly. Monday morning Martha comes up to me and tells me about the deal with Max. I responded, "Well does his auntie have COVID? "She shook her head no. Then, she said, "I should go down to medical and tell them that my boyfriend has COVID, so I don't have to go on the underway as well?" I said, "okay."

The next day is Tuesday. Martha ran up to me and said she went to medical and now she will be quarantined. I said, "Okay," she said you and Xavier should do it too. I said something like, "'no, thank you or, nah, I'm okay." She grabbed her stuff, and then she left.

I had duty on Wednesday. I went to the pier to give Xavier my extra bag of stuff that I didn't need onboard. Before I saw him, my chief came up to me and asked whether I was outside to see Martha. I said no. He said, "don't let Martha get you into trouble." I said, "yes, chief".

That Thursday was the last night we were going to be in port for roughly a month we were going to be underway. Martha had asked this girl in our cub to grab her shoes for her. That friendship did not sit right with me. Only because Martha kept calling her dirty and saying that she smelled. I was the one like, "well, I won't be trying to sniff her. She is a bit dirty and messy, but she's not that bad". Suddenly Martha goes cranking and this girl becomes like her new best friend. I just remember thinking she talked so much crap about her. Now, you two are the best of friends. What the heck? If you can speak wrong about her behind her back, become her best friend when you are around her; I wonder what you say and do behind my back. I thought that was so fake. I could not overlook that.

Martha asked the girl, and the girl told her FC1 had thrown her shoes away. Martha then asked me in an enormous paragraph basically, "why were my shoes thrown away?" I remember thinking, "who the fuck is she talking to? Nobody threw your shoes away. You need to ask your best friend to come and grab them for you because I'm not. She made me angry. First off, if you don't want anybody touching your shit, you should have been here or taken the shit with you. When I asked her what her shoe size was, she didn't know.

Martha then texted Xavier to grab her shoes for her. That vindictive little girl knew that he could not go into the female berthing. He asked me to hold it for her when he asked me to grab some food for him. I remember thinking, she asked you because I said no. I said, "Okay since I'm going to the pier to go get food now, let me get to Xavier's car." Max is in the front seat, and Martha is in the passenger seat. I get in the backseat. Max and Martha go back in forth. Max is saying he brought his uniform after two weeks of quarantine. They are going to be working somewhere temporary until the ship gets back. Then he says, "well if Ozlyn is nice enough, you can give her your key. And she can go grab your uniform for you." Martha acts like she didn't hear him. So, he repeats it. They both look back at me.

I was not in the mood. I was not about to do anything for Martha. And she already knew not to play with me. Xavier comes up to the car. He's like he just wanted food and a pair of his shoes from the berthing. I know it seemed like Max and Xavier had the same sort of arrangement. Max was borrowing Xavier's car for the next month. Max doing that favor for Xavier was the least he could do. Max explains to Xavier the plan. In addition, he keeps trying to tell Xavier to leave on his duty day. A big no-no here. We are not allowed to leave the ship on our duty day. If you do, you will be in big trouble. Xavier says "no" multiple times. Max says, "You're not going to get in trouble, I do it all the time." Xavier said, "No," and he left with his belongings.

Max asks me whether I can go grab the stuff for Martha. I said, "I don't want to make two trips. To go grab her stuff and then go grab the food. It's a long walk. Martha can go grab it herself." Then, Max says, "We're supposed to be quarantined. We can't go on the ship or let people see us. He then suggests while they go get the food. I go get Martha's uniform. By the time they come back. I should be back in uniform. I said "okay". That night I already knew it was going to be downhill from there.

Fast forward to the underway the next day. Everybody is talking about the stunt Max and Martha pulled. The dumbass they posted things on social media. They are out at the mall and not quarantined. Everyone was mad because we had to work twelve hours a day instead of eight hours for the first two weeks. That was the most selfish thing they could have done. That proved that they didn't care about anyone but themselves. They are both manipulative individuals.

The full underway everyone kept coming up to me asking questions. Then, they started mentioning that Martha and Max could be sent up to Captain's Mass for malingering. That is pretending to be sick, so you can get out of work. They would also get in trouble because you are supposed to be alone when you are quarantined. Isolated from society for two weeks. When medical contacted Max through FaceTime, Martha picked up the phone. There was more than enough evidence for them both to get held up. I felt like I had a heavy stone on my heart. This demonic individual is messing with my spirit. I could not bear to be her friend anymore.

Everyone is in combat from the last underway, getting ready for the underway or observing. Martha decides to go to her rack. She was gone for 45 minutes before they sent me to get her. OS2 Phillip asks me, "was she in the bathroom?" I said, "No." He asked me, "Was she in her rack?" I said, "She was in the berthing, but she wasn't in her rack."

OS2 Phillip didn't ask me any more questions. Martha was in the berthing in an empty rack. Which we are not allowed to do either. Then, after she gets in trouble, Jerry just made her sweep the ladder backs. She came up to me and said I should have lied. I was thinking you are cunning; I am not about to get in trouble for you. If you are bold enough to do the things you do, at least be woman enough to own up to it. She pissed me off that day. I never put her in a position where she had to lie for me and she was supposed to be my friend. Well, I think not.

As I said, I had all these problems weighing down on me. That wasn't my problem. They put a person on me that nobody else wanted to deal with. Everything she stood for went against my morals and ethics. I love to work. I am very independent. I am strong and I try not to lie. I try to be as kindhearted as possible and help others when I can. Martha could not be helped, and I am NOT my sister's keeper.

> I am NOT my sister's keeper.

That was my first time talking to chaps. He was right on time as if God knew what I was going through. I learned the lesson he had sent into my life. I promise you I felt like I had the weight of a stone on my heart. I was physically having trouble breathing. This girl was horrendous. What I found to be most shocking was everyone kept trying to make me babysit her. But no one wanted to take on the challenge. Nobody liked her. She was loud and annoying, overdramatic and she never did her job.

I cleaned off my plate with chaps. I felt a hundred times better. I had never felt like that before. Something so mentally draining made me feel physically drained. I felt like that girl was tugging on my spirit. That, I could not allow the devil to do. I cannot afford to get got. Therefore, Martha had to get away from me. I came to this ship by myself. I will leave this ship by myself. I am not my sister's keeper.

We were in Moorhead City. I ate Domino's Pizza that I ordered with the division. Things were great without Martha there. I trained and I didn't have to keep tabs on anyone. Once I got on watch, I didn't have to grab anyone to do their job. I didn't have to lie. I slept on my regular schedule. I didn't have to worry about dealing with something similar to an infant. Trying to distance my every move but simultaneously being a follower of others. Not having Martha on the underway was perfect.

Of course, we had to pull into home port when the underway finished. I think something else happened. I told Martha I did not want to be her friend. When we pulled in, Martha and Max were in medical getting yelled at. Nothing else came about, everything was simply swept under the rug.

I forgot to mention that Xavier had agreed with Max. The AC on his car would be fixed and some other things by the time we got back. Martha would select the cover on the bottom of his car. She messed it up when she hit a pothole. Max had also told Xavier that he didn't mean to get underway. He made it seem like it was an out-of-blue kind of thing. When Xavier said to me about their agreement and conversation, I told him, "Yea, he did mean to get out of the underway. He was nowhere near his auntie that weekend. Martha said his auntie didn't even have COVID."

Xavier asked me, how did I know?" I replied, "I asked Martha before she pulled her stunt and got quarantined."

Max pulled a whole scheme. The rest of the operations got the shitty end of the deal. Max and Martha used Xavier's car for an entire month, and they were quarantined at home in Max's barracks. They spent an ample amount of time hanging out and posting it on social media. Martha was being a follower. Max was being followed. I knew Max was trifling. I knew he was no good. I also began to realize he was a big liar.

Xavier said, "Now that makes me mad, and now I am pissed off." Honestly, it was too late. Two weeks had passed and we had two weeks left on the underway. For him to get mad now, was literally a waste of energy. I agreed he probably just wanted his car back. That big question was, what could make up for the manipulation? Did Max and Martha fulfill their end of the deal on fixing Xavier's car? The answer was emphatically, NO! They didn't.

Xavier had duty the day we pulled in, so I went to check into my barracks and grab him some Popeyes. I texted Max and asked him to take me. I specifically requested that he not bring Martha. I did not want to entertain her fake "oh, I missed you. You are my best friend show." I was not in the mood for it at all.

Max comes and picks me up. Does he ask me about the underway? About Xavier? I kept it brief I said, "it was good. I ain't got nothing to do with y'all agreement. I'm going to let y'all have y'all own conversation. I wasn't there and I don't know the specifics of what y'all agreed on. I'm just going to let y'all talk it out." He understood what it meant.

Suddenly, I asked him, "was he able to fix the AC? Did Martha fix the cover on the bottom of the car?" Max said, "I tried to get the AC fixed. I went to three different mechanics, they said they could not fix it because of the time of year. I tried to get his car re-registered, but Xavier had to do it himself. Martha did not fix his cover and I didn't know why. That's between Xavier and her."

Sounded like a load of crap to me. I never heard of an AC not being fixed because of the season. We were in Virginia. There was no reason for the two to not have fulfilled their end of the deal. Of course, he lied on the spot and said anything to try and make things go over smoothly. I mentioned that I couldn't be friends with Martha. In conclusion, she was not my friend and she was never my friend. I said, "this stunt of hers was the last straw."

He then commented, "Yea, I told her she should have gone underway instead of following me. Every time I tried to go out with friends or family, she just expected to tag along. I asked her, don't you have any friends of your own? I know I do. I can call them and get missing." He continued to say things like: he got tired of seeing her every day. It got boring quickly and she kept being clingy and just there. Unless he said, "let's go do something," she just wanted to be caged up all day.

In my mind I said, "this dirty dog. I cannot believe he just said that about her. I knew it." He changes up so quickly to match the energy in the room. He sat up there and was just lying in my face. The nerve of him. Martha just set herself up for failure, she acted like she had no idea what I meant when it came to Max. A long time ago, I just stopped giving her advice. I stopped trying to explain to her the red flags that surrounded Max. He talked a good game. When you listened to the words coming out of his mouth. The lies were blatantly obvious.

For example, he said he had an auntie that lived in the area, however; Max went out and when he came back, Martha was watching him from his room. He got out of the car and Martha saw him kissing a girl on the lips. She was so upset. He came into his room, but Martha didn't say anything. She just went outside, cried, and came back into the room extra sad and mopey. She finally asks him about the girl she saw him kissing on the lips.

Max said, "Congratulations, you passed! My auntie and I decided to test and make sure that if things are going wrong, are you just going to stay and work things out? Or are you going to be childish and up and leave? "

He said, "neither he nor his auntie saw her watching them from the parking lot. They decided to kiss on the lips to test her loyalty." Nobody is that gullible except Martha. She went along with the lie they made up and everything was okay afterward. Another example was when everybody needed to update their uniform. I brought it up to Martha that we should get our uniforms done together.

She said, "Max said that there was no way for our uniform to be sewed in in two days because everyone was fixing their uniform."

I remember thinking to myself about the whole situation. I had asked her a few days before she needed her uniform turned in on Wednesday. I had all of next weekend to get my uniform taken care of. She lets this man dictate her every mood and decision. Max said there was no way it could be done. That was the end of the story. She wasn't even going to try and she knew she needed it done.

Our chief told her to go to damage control because she had the whole week off from cranking. She did not go because she didn't want to. Three days into the week, she shows up at the ops office to see Max. Our chief asked her why she didn't do it. She lied and said she didn't know about it. He said, "yeah, you did because I specifically told you face to face that since you were off from the cranking, you were not off from the ship. You needed to take your ass to damage control."

I was in the damage control class. I asked her why she didn't go once he left. She said, "because I didn't want to. I was off from the galley. You honestly think I wanted to come back to the ship to work." She said, "come on now. I'm Martha. I do what I want and no, I don't get in trouble. "

She sounded stupid because she made her way back to the ship to sit underneath Max on his duty day. To sit in the ops office and watch them play the game. She could have done a lot of things instead of following a boy around. Max had his things taken care of at the end of every day. From the car ride with him to go get my barracks and the food. He thought she was very disposable.

He started to make her look like a fool. He never claimed her. He would always agree with the mean comments people said about her. He was terrible. When I had a phone conversation with my auntie, I kept mentioning how they were and their traits. They are both big liars, manipulators, entitled, selfish and just toxic people. That is what made them perfect for each other.

Xavier got his car back. He was mad. He let Max manipulate him out of not being angry. I, however; was not taking any chances. I was starting to see things clear as day. This undesignated seaman named Earl came upstairs to the operations. I never really talked to him before this. I remember seeing him a few times in my repair locker. He is horrid. His face is just weird. He gave off this energy that he worked hard and he was excited to strike a rate. He seemed like he wasn't a problematic person. I didn't know for sure. Earl and I were cordial acquaintances.

Chapter 3 Part 2: Furthermore

November 1st, 2020

Dear Diary,

I'll pray. *"Dear God, of course I am not struggling to trust you. I trust you 100%. Every word of yours, I believe. You are always on time because You are who You are. You never give us more than we can handle. I believe in You from the bottom of my heart; I do. I have faith, and I pray for guidance, strength, courage, integrity, and intelligence. I pray to be alert in the presence of the devil, but I just can't be alert enough with Martha. She is the devil in sheep's clothes. She needs help that I can't give her. I am sure God put her in my life as a lesson. Amen."*

Tomorrow, we pull into the port. Thank God! He is always good, putting us where we need to be. God is always loving and cheering us. I had to talk to Max tomorrow. I don't care about Martha. I am riding with Max tomorrow to clear and clean the air between us. I'm going to get my barracks room tomorrow, set my hair appointment, and grab Xavier some Popeyes. Xavier's on duty, so, of course he's upset. I like him so much. And I was thinking about writing a letter. The same thing I did with my mom; how I tried to clear things up. In retrospect, maybe I should just ask Xavier why he is upset with me. I'm going to wait till we are alone. We don't have to sugar coat our conversation.

I'm not mad at Martha. I'm done. I washed my hands of her. I'm focusing on myself. I love myself, my friends, my family, my life, and she does not fall into any of those categories.

~ R.E.O. ~

November 2nd, 2020

Dear Diary,

I am finally at the port, and it feels so good. I finally got a barracks room. Yes! I love it. I am very grateful. Xavier is amazing, I just want to take things slow. I'm tired. I'm glad to be on the porch and I'm going to go to bed.

~ R.E.O. ~

November 11th, 2020

Dear Diary,

Happy Veterans Day! It's my first one while active and I got duty today. Things will always be great, even though I broke things off with Xavier. We are just friends and there is nothing wrong with that. I just realized that he doesn't want to commit to me. We were practically dating and he was calling it something else. According to him we were only talking. Now it's just that he likes me, but we only work together. I would rather end things on a positive note rather than a negative one. I like Xavier and I wish he felt the same way, but in life we don't always get what we want. I want him. Other than that, it was a couple of days ago when I gathered all of my things from Xavier's room and put them in mine.

Today, I found out that this other guy likes me. He is okay, not anything like Xavier, but I'll see how things work out. The issue is, he is friends with another guy that likes me. Before I got to the ship, I hung out with that guy a few times and Lord knows it wouldn't be a great idea. I don't make friends. If I am seeing you, I'm not going to see your friends or anyone you are close with. In addition to that, it feels like he just wanted to hook up and I'm not interested in hooking up with anyone.

~ R.E.O. ~

November 22, 2020

Dear Diary,

I know it has been a few days, but I've been asking the question to Xavier and he doesn't want to give me the label. Xavier said it's not because he doesn't want to; it's because he is not ready. I appreciate the honesty and that's probably because this other guy didn't; he broke my heart. So, I'm interested in taking things slow. I am up for it. He is right about taking it slow. Anyway, Xavier and I are good. I am giving him some time to himself. I like him. I can honestly see myself with him.

Anyway, you know how I am - always itching for success and now, I got my career ladder. I'm climbing and you better be there with me. In conclusion, I washed my hands with Martha. Nothing else to say. I am sure of that. Do you know when I'll get my ESWS? I can't get it right now and I'm bummed about that.

~ R.E.O. ~

November 24th, 2020

Dear Diary,

A group of us went to Richard's house and met Kayla's family. It was beautiful. Reminded me of my crazy family back home. They argued about basketball. We had a dancing night. We blasted music and joked. All in all, we had a great night. I had duty on Thanksgiving but wasn't upset or anything. I had partied so late the night before that I slept in on Thanksgiving after turnover. I met my divo later on the mess decks. She sat and ate chow with me and another OS. We went back for seconds because there was so much food. Couldn't let it go to waste. Things were great. I had and have so much to be thankful for.

~ R.E.O. ~

December 1st, 2020

Dear Diary,

It is the last month of the year. Xavier and I are fine. I told him about something from my past, something I wouldn't have put on paper, ever in my life. The moral of the story was that I was shocked when I scared him away a bit. But I said what I said. I don't know why he reacted the way he did, but I'm marking it as a red flag.

~ R.E.O. ~

December 3rd, 2020

Dear Diary,

I patched things up with Xavier, that's my baby right there. Today was a great day. We are in port and we are finishing the underway tomorrow. I was angry that they sent me cranking because the holidays start soon. Then the holiday stands down. I am going to a Waffle House with Kayla. When we get back, I have some things I want to do and try. I planned for all the things I planned to do on deployment.

~ R.E.O. ~

December 12th, 2020

Dear Diary,

I got sent cranking to replace Martha. I was upset in the beginning because Martha hadn't finished her time. They were just so sick and tired of her. They did not want to deal with her. They already had their annoying little twit. They did not want another one. We were underway when this happened. I was told a few days prior that I would be going cranking on this date, so I had time to prepare. I told my watch group that I was leaving. and that Martha would replace me on my watch. Nobody was happy that she was coming back, including Max. Well, at least he tagged along with the views of everyone else.

There was an officer on our watch time. He seemed cool, but he was messy. He decided to ask Max about Heather. He said, "Max, aren't you the baby daddy to Heather?" Max said, "no, Heather and I were good friends. She is pregnant, but I am not the father. We were never on a level like that." It sounded like a robotic response that was practiced on a monotone level.

I'm thinking... if Max and Heather were good friends like he claims they were, then when Heather came on board, and she was clearly showing, why didn't Max pull his really good friend aside and squash the rumors? Instead, he was completely silent. He had nothing to say about anything, until we all pulled out into the middle of the ocean with no internet connection. Heather isn't here, and she has no way of responding to his comments. Max is just something else.

Moving on. I go cranking on December 12th. I go to the quarters with S-2, but before quarters she tries to come and talk to me. I walked away while she was talking mid-sentence. I was just pissed. It's bad enough that you get out of doing your damn job. Don't come to sit in my face like you are sincere about throwing me under the bus. Every time she falls short of doing her job, am I supposed to fill in and get the job done? I think you've done enough. Get the fuck away from me. Go back to the division. Get out of my face!

I got training from another FSA, not Martha. Usually, the person getting relieved is supposed to train the person sent to replace them. Martha never did her 90 days of cranking. She did maybe a month and a half. We both checked in and out separately. She got missing. Maybe she was skating. I don't know what she was doing. I had the watch from 0800 to 1200. We were checking in at 0800. When lunchtime rolls around, Martha makes her way to the mess decks at 1030. She is trying to eat lunch as if she is still cranking. I was pissed. She never did her job cranking. She is supposed to be taking over my watch. We replaced each other. She was supposed to be on my watch the 08 to 12, not skating and being on the mess decks.

I dumped my tray and I called to combat. I'm like, "isn't Martha supposed to be on my watch? Didn't we replace each other? Why is she chilling on the mess decks eating lunch?" He said, "yea, she is supposed to be on your watch. I've been waiting for her to come up all morning." I swear the amount of hatred I have toward this lazy broad built up so much and so fast.

I go up to her, and I asked her. "Aren't you supposed to be on my watch?" So she tries to lie to me and tell me that Chief told her that she didn't have to go on watch. I said, "well, I called so and so, and he said you are supposed to be on watch right now." She wasn't training me. She was just doing absolutely nothing. Not her job, nothing and I was mad. You did everything you could to get kicked out of cranking. Now that you are, you are trying to play both sides of the coin. I already know how cunning and vindictive she is. I am not about to let her pull a fast one on me.

She dumps her tray, and she goes on her watch. The next thing I saw was this girl named Lola, who she became friends with while she was down there. While I was serving, I saw Martha in the corner talking to many people who were cranking, including Lola. She is talking to them. I see her making gestures in my direction, plus they are all looking at me. Martha was over there telling them what had happened.

Ten minutes later, Lola comes over to where I am serving pizza. She comments, "It smells stank over here." I looked at her cause she was standing on my right. She didn't even look up at me. She stood there and continued to grab food. Martha had already tried throwing me under the bus before. This was the first time she had involved other people. I was pissed I wanted to slap the shit out of that stupid bitch.

I brought attention to the issue that I was having. I did not appreciate that this little girl wanted to play the victim. She never does what the fuck she is supposed to be doing. She dares to pass it on to other people as if what she's doing is okay. While I am conversing about it, I find out that Lola made claims that the reason she moved from my cube was because she felt uncomfortable around me. She claimed she felt as though I was watching her when she was getting dressed. The only problem was we were never in the berthing together. I never saw her take a shower; she had never seen me go shower nor get dressed. We were hours apart in our schedule.

I remember being so upset. This demonic person kept trying to play me like a fool. Then, to top it off she always played stupid every time I confronted her about it. I was beginning to not be able to stand her. Martha needed to be a follower. She could never stand on her own. She never had a voice of her own.

December 13th, 2020

Dear Diary,

     My legs hurt as if I just got off an eight-hour shift from Walgreens. I have been working since 8 o'clock. My patience is wearing thin with this bitch. We will never be cool again unless we fight it out. Hell Nah! I am so tired tonight.

~ R.E.O. ~

December 14th, 2020

Dear Diary,

     I talked to Xavier about Martha. She is bad news and just as I said, we will never be cool again. That is exactly why I wash my hands of her. I'm done with the whole thing. The only thing I want, is to not be bothered.

~ R.E.O. ~

December 15th, 2020

"Stop letting people who do so little for you control so much of your mind, feelings, and emotions."

"Stop letting people who do so little for you control so much of your mind, feelings, and emotions."

~ Will Smith ~

Dear Diary,

I have my blue jacket at a quarter board today. It went great. I was nervous, but I had a new experience. I am so excited to be on the ship serving my country. I wanted to spend time with Xavier, but I was a part of the skeleton crew. There is no way he can sneak into my room, but maybe the element of surprise is better? He is the apple of my eye. He said he wanted to do something nice for me, so I want him to be able to. Being in the cheese messes is great. I don't like the food served in the shoe. Pleasing people is not my thing.

~ R.E.O. ~

December 23rd, 2020

Dear Diary,

     I am always doing perfectly fine. Especially since I am officially a third-class petty officer, of course. I am so proud of myself and as always, I love myself. Around this time, I always love bringing up Xavier. Lately, things have been really good. We hung out with some friends and spent the night at their house. We are dog-sitting. He is such a great guy. I want him in my future. I care about him a lot and I know he cares about me. I am falling for him. I don't have to keep saying it to know it. He is the only person I see myself with. He is my favorite "piece of chocolate," and it is what I nicknamed him. I was getting upset about my credit score, but now I am planning to have great credit by the end of deployment. In addition to saving my money. I love you. Have a great night.

~ R.E.O. ~

I went cranking on December 12th to replace Martha. She did not finish her time cranking. She kept being a problem child and got sent back to the division early. Do you know who else came back early from cranking? Max. We already know what monkey sees monkey does at this point. I was upset because she never did her job. Then, they always send me to do it. I was starting to get tired of her at this point.

At least I was told a few days prior, so I let my watch team know that I was going cranking soon. Nobody was happy. Everybody was like, "what the fuck!" Martha had just pulled the October underway thing with Max. She didn't go up to Captains' Mass for it. Now, she didn't even make up the month she wasn't cranking. She just got off because they didn't want to deal with her.

I figured if I just did my job and did not complain, things would be okay. I was keeping an open mind. I didn't have much time to write. I was waking up at 4:30 in the morning and was getting off at 1830. I was beyond tired and I was hitting my rack.

December 16th, 2020

"You are stronger than you think. You have gotten through every bad day in your life, and. You are undefeated."

~ M. A. ~

December 19th, 2020

Dear Diary,

You are strong.

You are beautiful.

You are loved.

You are special.

You are not weak.

You are not flawed.

You are not weird.

You are not a lost cause.

Honestly, I have no idea if I wrote this or if this is a quote from the motivational app.

December 20th, 2020

"When someone isn't treating you right, no matter how much you love them, you've got to love yourself more and walk away."

~ M. A. ~

December 21st, 2020

"Finding your passion isn't just about careers and money. It's about finding your authentic self. The one you've buried beneath other people's needs."

~ Anonymous ~

December 22nd, 2020

I got my hair washed and silk pressed. Xavier and I were dog-sitting. As time passed, I was hanging with Xavier, we got close and enjoyed each other's company. We also hung out with Richard and his wife, Kayla.

~ R.E.O. ~

December 23rd, 2020

"Some people aren't loyal to you. They are loyal to their need of you. Once their needs change, so does their loyalty."

~ M. A. ~

December 24th, 2020

Dear Diary,

I worked this day. I went to the barracks and chilled. I didn't ask Xavier to pick me up because I could have gotten called in on Christmas. I didn't want him to make the forty-minute drive back and forth. No one was delivering food, that was the only bummer. On Christmas, Xavier picked me up around 1500. We spent Christmas with Parker and his family, Deborah, and the kids. It was nice. I had a great time. I would go buy McDonald's, but Deborah had cooked food. They offered food to us and we hung out, chatted, and listened to music. Then, we headed back to finish dog sitting for our friends.

~ R.E.O. ~

December 28th, 2020

"Unconditional love is when someone hurts you, but because you care about that person so much, you choose not to hurt them in return."   ~ M. A.~

I was binge-watching *America's Next Top Model*. I was chilling and relaxing.

~ R.E.O. ~

December 29th, 2020

"As I look back on my life, I realize that every time I thought I was being rejected for something good, I was being redirected to something better."

~ Steve Maraboli ~

December 29th, 2020

"Respect yourself enough to know you deserve the very best."

~ M. A. ~

December 30th, 2020

Dear Diary,

Today, I had a conversation with Martha. A fucking headache is what it gave me.

~ R.E.O. ~

December 31st, 2020

Dear Diary,

I went to work. When I was off work, my two-week vacation began. I got dropped off at my hotel room by Xavier and we were supposed to drop Fred off at the airport, but he changed his mind. I caught my plane ride to Florida the next day.

~ R.E.O. ~

Chapter 4: A Four-Shadow of Betrayal

"If you want 2021 to be your year:

Go out make a change.'

Smile more

Be excited

Do new things

Show more gratitude.

Do things that challenge you.

Be brave."

~ M. A. ~

January 1st, 2021

Dear Diary,

I took a plane ride to Florida.

"2021 is the beginning of anything you want."

~ M. A. ~

January 2nd, 2021

"You know it's love when all you want is that person to be happy, even if you're not part of their happiness."

~ Julia Roberts ~

Dear Diary,

Back home, looking over my things, I ran across the letters and the notes I kept from boot camp. My favorite part were the notes to myself.

"**16-FEB-20**: Note to Self: Live life because you moved back home and ended up in Tallahassee alone. Explore the world and visit home. Don't feel bad. Live!"

"**20-FEB-20**: Note to Self: You are tough! You are strong! Run with heart and soul. You've got this! You can't get there by walk-in. 4 mins or 4 weeks! It's only temporary!"

"**23-FEB-20**: Note to Self: You got this! Why are you here?? To be a sailor. You… are a sailor. Finish what you started, Ozlyn!"

"**25-FEB-20**: Note to Self: Remember when you thought you weren't ready to swim. They made you jump off the tower. You swam – so very proud of you! I love you!"

"**01-MAR-20**: Note to Self: Warrior mindset obtained. Let's finish what we started. Pass our P.F.A. and get back on track. Thank you, Jesus!"

"**04-MAR-20**: Note to self: You can only go up from here. Life is a journey; this is yours. Live and enjoy. I am so proud of you. I am so proud of us. I love you."

Note to self: You can only go up from here.

"**07-MAR-20:** Note to self: I love my family. I want them to be taken care of. The major plan initiates in one more week… I am so proud of you! I love you!"

"**14-MAR-20**: Great job! We did it! We are in the Navy! Yes, Lord! Our Heavenly Father gave us strength. Don't stop and can't stop!"

~ R.E.O. ~

January 4th, 2021

"You are worth more than second thoughts and maybes…"

~ M. A. ~

January 5th, 2021

"Anyone can give you attention and compliments…but someone who loves you will give you that plus respect, honesty, trust, and loyalty."

~ Charles J. Orlando ~

January 6th, 2021

"Remind yourself of what you have been able to overcome. All the times you felt like you weren't going to make it through, you proved yourself wrong. You are more powerful than you think."   ~ Ash Alves ~

Dear Diary,

When I was on leave, I had so much fun. I was doing TikTok with my family. I did a photoshoot in my uniform for my first anniversary in the Navy. I had a Publix chicken tender sub, yummy! On my last day of leave, my family had an indoor strip club party for me. My plane ride back to Virginia was on the 10th of January. All the fun had come to an end.

January 10th, 2021

"Stay focused, ignore the distractions, and you will accomplish your goals much faster."

                                                            ~ M. A. ~

Dear Diary

My plane ride was early. I had a full day ahead of me, so I went to the Virginia Aquarium with my friend Kayla. Afterward we went to a seafood restaurant called 'Mr. Boil' and the food was magnificent. This restaurant made me put together a bucket list of restaurants to try in Virginia.

~ Later that day~

Dear Diary,

I did not write any entries for the New Year, but I was very busy with everyone and enjoying every day of my leave. I like it in the Navy and congrats to me on my one-year anniversary of being in the Navy. I love it. Today I went to the Virginia Aquarium with Kayla, and it was so much fun. Kayla is a great friend to have as company. She is just someone with good vibes. Other than that, I start work tomorrow. I'm going to get back on my grind harder and better than ever.

                                                            ~ R.E.O. ~

January 14th, 2021

"If you only knew how much those little moments with you mattered to me."

~ M. A. ~

Dear Diary,

Six Important Guidelines in Life:

1. When you are alone, mind your thoughts.
2. When you are with friends, mind your tongue.
3. When you are angry, mind your temper.
4. When you are with a group, mind your behavior.
5. When you are in trouble, mind your emotions.
6. When God starts blessing you, mind your ego.

January 16th, 2021

Dear Diary,

Richard had a game night with his friends. Xavier and I went together. Parker and his wife (Deborah) showed up together. The hosts were Richard and Kayla.

January 18th, 2021

"I'm selfish, impatient, and a little insecure. I make mistakes; I am out of control and, at times, hard to handle. But if you can't handle me at my worst, then you sure as hell don't deserve me at my best."

~ Marilyn Monroe ~

Dear Diary,

Happy Martin Luther King Day. Today was hot and cold. Today, Xavier broke my heart. I never thought he would do what he did. Xavier snitched on himself. He went back home and slept with a girl. He even talked down upon me to justify his actions, I can't believe it. I am disappointed and speechless. This is the second time he chose another girl. Other than that, it was also a girls' night out. We got our toes done together and went to a restaurant and chatted. We ended the night by going to the sex store.

~ R.E.O. ~

January 23rd, 2021

"Things will get better, and you need to trust in that."

~ M. A. ~

The color of my soul is pink. Affectionate and loving, it's easy for you to care about everyone. You want the world to be a kinder place for everyone, and you do your part to help those in need. You're an angel that spreads love and positivity around the world.

January 24th, 2021

"True love stands by each other's side on good days and stands closer on bad days."
~ M. A. ~

Dear Diary,

I went roller skating with Richard and Kayla. I was missing Xavier, but he had duty. I had a lot of fun, though. ~
R.E.O. ~

January 25th, 2021

Dear Diary,

I feel like I haven't written in a while, but everything is great. Xavier mentioned moving in together. After we talked, I asked him again if he wanted to be with me and he said yes. We were okay, so I'm thinking about it. I didn't say yes, but I'm thinking about it. After deployment, I think I will make Kayla my best friend. But so far, I've been organizing my rack and I have everything I need for deployment. Things are great.

I do plan to move into my place at the end of this year, I'm just working things out to be able to do that. The C.O. is making history. I am so happy to be on this platform. I've been setting up my rack and I pretty much got everything I needed. I consider it a compliment that I am always getting compared to the C.O. I think people see a vision that I see. I know it's going to happen one day.

~ R.E.O. ~

January 29th, 2021

Dear Diary,

Xavier and I talked. Once again, I asked and clarified if he wanted to be with me. We were in his car and were having a conversation about everything. I wanted his honesty. I wanted to make the most out of our time together. It had started snowing in Virginia. We were back to being good again; we had a date night with some friends. We took pictures and enjoyed ourselves.

~ R.E.O. ~

February 1st, 2021

"I'm thankful for all those difficult people in my life; they have shown me exactly whom I don't want to be."

~ M. A. ~

Dear Diary,

I am so excited about my promotion because I can see the increase in money. Just gives me great help for the future. I am so ready for this deployment. Today was pretty good. Now I am in bed right. Tomorrow, I am going to go fix my uniform. Xavier forgot, and he was tired. That is fine. Life goes on.

~ R.E.O. ~

February 2nd, 2021

"Cutting someone completely off from your life is sometimes necessary for your peace. Don't feel guilty about it." ~ M. A. ~

February 3rd, 2021

"Dream like Martin,

Lead like Harriet,

Fight like Malcolm,

Think like Garvey,

Write like Maya,

Build like Madam C.J,

Speak like Fredrick,

Educate like W.E.B.,

Believe like Thurgood,

Challenge like Rosa"

~ M. A. ~

Dear Diary,

I bought Xavier a Nintendo Switch. He was shocked, but yeah, I am a giver. I didn't think it was too soon. He kept talking about Max being stingy with his Switch. He would play it with everyone except for Xavier. Then, he would make excuses and put it up when Xavier wanted to play. I believe that Max had no right to be upset with Xavier. Considering that Xavier let him borrow his car for a whole month, Max lied and didn't do anything to the car that he promised to fix. Max was never his friend and for him to act funny nowadays, is not right. It seemed like a bitch move for him. Anyhow, I am super tired. Night!   ~R.E.O. ~

February 4th, 2021

"Take a moment now to stop and thank yourself for how far you've come. You've been trying to make changes in your life, and all your effort count."

~ Karen Salmansohn ~

Dear Diary,

The Richards had a date night with Xavier and me. I called my little sister on FaceTime so she could see. We ate at Applebee's, and I had never eaten there before. We all took pictures together. I enjoyed my night. It was the highlight of my happiness, especially because Xavier and I were together. We looked good. Little did I know it wasn't real. It never was, and it never would be.

~ R.E.O. ~

February 5th, 2021

Dear Diary,

I face-timed my family and today was Parker's Birthday. It was so lovely. We jammed until the neighbors came to complain about the music. His wife, Deborah, asked me a very odd question. She said, "If my husband is doing anything on deployment. You would let me know, right?"

I found it very weird. Especially when she asked me at the restaurant when we went out on girls' night. I already told her they don't talk about that stuff around me. When she asked me, I said in the heat of the moment, "sure. Yeah. I'll tell you." I brought my polaroid camera to take pictures. We sang happy birthday to Parker. We all were eating cake and drinking alcohol. We wrapped the night up with a neat bow.

February 6th, 2021

Dear Diary,

Around 5 in the morning, I got a phone call from Deborah. She is crying and being so hysterical on the phone, saying Parker was fighting her. He took the keys from her. She and the children couldn't get in the house. She wanted me or somebody on the ship to grab the keys so she could head out of town, so when she gets back from out of town, they'll be able to get into their apartment. I told her I wasn't on duty. Xavier and Richard were. I would let them know so they could help her out. I felt so bad for her.

The boys confronted Parker about it. He said, "no." They told me there was nothing else they could do. So, they suggested I leave it alone. I told Deborah the situation and she said, "cool." In the morning, she would just wait for the leasing office to open at 10 a.m. She just wanted to get on the road as quickly as possible. I told her if there was anything else she needed, I was there. That was the end of that conversation.

I was chilling with my friend's dog and hanging out with Kayla. We grabbed McDonald's for her husband, Richard. Xavier doesn't eat at McDonald's and he didn't want food. He asked me to grab his crows for his uniform instead. Later that day, we had dinner with Kayla's coworkers at Buffalo Wild Wings. It ended up being very delicious. I had an Oreo Blizzard from Dairy Queen for dessert.

February 7th, 2021

Dear Diary,

This was the day we all had to go to the hotel to quarantine. Richard found out on the way there that he wasn't going on deployment. This broke my heart a bit. He is hilarious and just a fun person to be around and work with. It was in his best interest and I was happy he got to stay back with Kayla. It was just bittersweet.

February 12th, 2021

Dear Diary,

I let my family know about my deployment address. The whole time I was quarantined in the hotel, I was relaxed. I redid my plaits. Uber eats was on delivery twice a day because I was ordering food. I had a photo session and did the silhouette challenge on TikTok. I was messaging Xavier, but he was acting funny. I couldn't pinpoint it. I thought he was chilling just like me in the room. He asked to come to my hotel room, but I said, "no, I didn't want to get in trouble." I was thinking we both just made rank and I don't want us to get demoted two paygrades. I was thinking of our best interest.

~ R.E.O. ~

February 13th, 2021

Dear Diary,

I knew my hotel stay was coming to an end. I spent time downloading a lot of music from Spotify to my phone. I downloaded books as well. I fell in love with the Chinese Shar-Pei, also known as the Hippo dog. This will be my dog as soon as I am on shore duty.

~ R.E.O. ~

February 14th, 2021

"You meet thousands of people, and none of them touch you. And then you meet one person, and your life is changed forever."

~ Love and Other Drugs ~

Dear Diary,

Happy Valentine's Day. I love myself so much. I think last Valentine's Day I was in boot camp. I am officially on a self-love journey. The first thing that happened this morning was that I saw Xavier and he said hi to me. Then he up and disappeared before I had a chance to say anything else. I felt something was off, but I'm ready to get back to work and focus on deployment. Self-love day number one is about "what is one thing you love about yourself?" I am a giver, genuine person and in addition to that; I love myself. My self-love always has room for improvement. I am human, so I am not perfect. I can continuously improve in the name of the Lord Jesus Christ, my Lord, and my Savior.

This was the day the entire ship was checking out of the hotel. Deployment was officially commencing on Valentine's Day. After I turned in my room key, I joined everyone in the ballroom area. Xavier said "Hi" to me. He saw me before I had a chance to notice him. When I dropped my things and lifted my head to speak to him, he disappeared. I thought that was so strange. I was hoping he would have said, "Happy Valentine's Day," but he didn't.

I gave him the benefit of the doubt and thought the day had just begun. He never said anything else to me. It felt like he was keeping his distance. The situation dawned on me, but I was about to go back to work cranking. Working from 0430 to 1800. I didn't have the time to confront him and ask about it.

Just the thought of going back made me tired, so I took a nap. I hit my rack, and CS3 was mad because I missed most of the meal. I had to make up for that first mistake and work twice as hard.

~ R.E.O. ~

February 15th, 2021

"I'm thankful for my struggle because, without it, I wouldn't have stumbled across my strength."

~ Alex Elle ~

February 16th, 2021

Dear Diary,

These last couple of days have been hectic, but I like it. Also, I'm so worked out. I am tired. I added things to my collage in my rack.

~ R.E.O. ~

February 17th, 2021

"You – and only you – are ultimately responsible for whom you become and how happy you are."   ~ Rachel Hollis ~

Dear Diary,

Today was great. I have 22 days left cranking. It feels good. It feels great; thank you, Jesus.

~ R.E.O. ~

February 18th, 2021

"If someone makes you miserable more than they make you happy, then it is time to let them go, no matter how much you love them."   ~ M. A. ~

Dear Diary,

I have 21 days left cranking. Tomorrow, I think I have to go do breakouts before I leave. So far, so good and I am excited for day five. I got my passport today. Yay!   ~ R.E.O. ~

February 19th, 2021

"Nothing annoys me more than when someone expects you to be okay with something that they wouldn't be okay with if you did it."

~ M. A. ~

Dear Diary,

Today was good. We got Marines, and they are a big help. I am so excited. I have 21 days left. On another note, today's self-love day is number four.

February 20th, 2021

"The wrong one will find you in peace and leave you in pieces, but the right one will find you in pieces and lead you to peace."

~ Unknown ~

Today I found the perfect quote. It said, *"The wrong one will find you at peace and leave you in pieces, but the right one will find you in pieces and lead you to peace."* Oh, I love this quote. This was meant for Xavier and me. I am freaking in love with this quote. I found Xavier in a bad place and now he is happy. He is less angry and always on time to work. He got his shit together. Wow, I love this! Today was good. I've got 19 days left. Self-love day number seven is to kill the comparison habit.

> *"The wrong one will find you at peace and leave you in pieces, but the right one will find you in pieces and lead you to peace."*

I found this quote on TikTok from @secandaho. He said his interpretation was that *"You are the right one to put yourself together and make yourself better than before! You are the one to save yourself, to help yourself, to be there for yourself."* I disagreed with his logic at first. I thought the quote was about Xavier and me. I wasn't interpreting the whole meaning of the quote because Xavier was in pieces when I found him. I led him to peace. I wasn't in pieces when he found me. I was at peace. Based on the quote, Xavier was going to leave me in pieces. Was Xavier the wrong one?

~ R.E.O. ~

February 21st, 2021

Dear Diary,

I now have 18 days left of cranking. Feels good. Today was pretty good, just long. I have to be back at 4 a.m. Oh my gosh! I am almost at the finish line. We are going to Morehead to pick up our counterparts. Today I'm going to miss eating decently, you know… but whatever. I need to become OS2. I've got to focus on the bigger picture.

~ R.E.O. ~

February 22nd, 2021

Dear Diary,

HOW I FOUND OUT.

This is the day I found out the truth about what was up with Xavier. This girl that started cranking, her name was Priscilla, I heard about her a little bit. I knew she was bad news. Nobody likes her. She said, "I would have a mentor and then they would always quit on me."

I felt bad for her when I heard her say that. I didn't want to be her friend. I remember telling Kayla about her; I told her I wanted to be cordial with Pricilla and help her feel less alone.

Kayla told me, "Oz if everybody leaves her alone after a while, I don't want you to find out why in a bad way. "I agreed with Kayla. I told her I noticed she likes to draw, so I'm just going to be sharing a little of my artwork with her. That's it. I had no clue concerning why nobody messed with Priscilla. I had to find out the hard way.

Just like I said, Priscilla started cranking in the pot shack. I kept our interactions simple and short. We were cranking together and everybody ate together before the meal. During the meal we would all be working. I quickly realized that Priscilla was ugly. She was. She was loud, rude, and had no filter. Deep down, you could tell she was lonely. She tended to want to be the center of attention a lot. She was always getting into trouble as well. She was a big liar and she just wanted attention. A lot of it.

All of that seems harmless, I guess. I kept my distance. Multiple people told me not to hang around her. Don't even sit with her. You know when you feed a wild animal and they keep coming back? That's how she was acting. I knew to listen when Priscilla tried to spread a couple of lies about me. I was completely dumbfounded and taken back a bit. I started stepping back big time. I always found her staring and looking at me. She was like a psycho, honestly. She was weird. She was just bad news. Her jokes were stupid and wild. It was cringy being around her.

For instance, this one morning, I had to work with a different cook. I was joking with him and I was singing, "Are you ready for this? (humming)" when she overheard our conversation, Priscilla said, "Oz, all your enthusiasm makes me want to punch you in the face." I'm thinking, what? Like why the fuck would you even say that? She was unstable.

Anyway, this one evening, we were all sitting down to eat dinner before the meal. She invited me to go smoke weed with her and another shipmate. I said, "no, thank you. I'm not interested." She asked, "why?" I said, "I have never smoked marijuana and I never will." She said, "why? The whole time I was at the hotel smoking with my mentor in my room." I asked, "who's your mentor?" She said, "OS2 Xavier." And pointed at him across the room.

He was grabbing something to drink. When she pointed, he disappeared quickly. She wasn't loud enough for him to hear us because we were way across the room. He knew the truth was slowly coming out. Xavier looked me in my eyes before he sped up and walked out of there. I had to go serve because the meal had started.

I had to know the truth because it just couldn't be true. Right? I mean the only thing I asked Xavier for was his honesty. He was so honest; that was the very first thing I liked about him. We talked and we had an agreement that if you don't want to be with me, then just say that. We understood each other because I told him multiple times that there are guys who are interested in me. If you don't want to be with me, just say it. Do you know how many of his friends or guys, in general, have asked me for my number? I shut them all down because I was with Xavier. I was more than willing to leave Xavier if he did not want to be with me. It's been six months. He didn't communicate anything of the sort.

I was shocked and I had to know the truth. I got advice from my buddy. He said, "Fuck that bitch! You need to go set her ass straight and tell her that's your man. You need answers. What the fuck is she talking about?"

(Side note: CS3 was my boy, shout-out to Kentucky State University! They got a real one going there. #Shrek&Donkey)

He permits me to leave, so I do. I confront her passively. I'm picking up a pot and asking her, "What did you mean you were in the hotel room smoking with your mentor? What was going on? Who came to whose room?"

She tells me everything. Xavier went to her room. I asked her to see the messages. She shows me. I'm like, "Xavier and I are together." I swear the truth was in front of me in black and white. After I double-checked the phone numbers. I needed to find Xavier and rip his fucking face off. I was livid. I started putting on my game face. The whole time Priscilla started shouting and telling people, "We bout to go catch a fuckboi." She was loud, putting the situation out there for everyone. I said, "no, I'm going to go confront him. Will you keep this between us?"

I start hunting. The first place I checked, he was there, taking a nap. I woke his ass the fuck up. I was so heated. I asked to speak to him in the corner. You know that moment where your parents are so disappointed and you stand there with that stupid ass look on your face because you don't know what to say. That was Xavier's facial expression. I was trying to contain my anger, so my responses were coming out slowly but surely.

"You and Priscilla?" "At the hotel, huh." "You went to her room." "Smoked weed" "You wanted to fuck and "She said, no." "That's the only reason." "Because you also didn't have." "A condom, huh?" He was speechless.

The amount of betrayal was overwhelming, all plastered on my face. If I wasn't at work, I could have killed him. Everything started to make sense. The guilty behavior. He avoided me for two weeks straight. Usually, he would go out of his way to check on me. He was acting so strange. I'm over here upset because he didn't say Happy Valentine's Day to me. That wasn't even the bigger picture. My last line to Xavier was, "I'm done."

I walked away. When I exited the room, my world was crashing, spinning, and burning because it was all overwhelming. I remember telling myself, I can't forgive him. I can't take him back. I can't. I can't give him the benefit of the doubt. I can't give him any more chances. The first person I called was Kayla. Kayla picked up on the first ring. She was preaching to me. She was there for me when I needed her most. I was completely blindsided.

Where did this come from? I'm thinking about the words he said to me. He was reassuring me that I wasn't going to lose him. He asked me to move in with him and he was talking about having a kid with me some day. I was remembering how we were together the night before deployment started. He was laying in my lap, talking to me, and cuddling with me. I had no idea.

That's why Kayla takes the award for my best friend. Everybody betrayed me and Xavier was the last piece of the puzzle.

The other person I wanted to kill was Martha. So, I want to make it clear that Priscilla got around. She was easy and accessible to everyone. Priscilla was originally talking to Max. Martha got jealous and she told Max to stop talking to Priscilla around the time we went to the hotel. Priscilla was in the same duty section with Max, Xavier, and Parker. Parker sent out a group chat with Xavier and Priscilla. Martha told Priscilla that Xavier wasn't seeing anyone. That's the only reason Priscilla and Xavier ever started talking. When Priscilla asked Martha, "is Xavier seeing anyone?" Martha told her, "no." I know Martha has no obligation to me, but when Priscilla asked me was Max seeing someone?" I told her, "Yes, he is, and I wouldn't bark up that tree."

Martha is a slimy-ass bitch. Priscilla was interested in Reece. She was also interested in a marine guy. She wrote love letters to him, professing her love for him and everything. I was so upset that those six months with Xavier were wasted. I can never get that time or energy back. Of course, I could never erase those memories. Xavier made me happy once upon a time. I had to find out the hard way that happiness is temporary and joy is everlasting. Xavier did not bring me joy; he made me question my happiness. These are the scriptures from my friend Kayla.

Proverbs 16:9.

> "In their hearts, humans plan their course, but the Lord establishes their steps."

Proverbs 16:20.

> "Whoever gives heed to instruction prospers and blessed is the one who trusts in the lord."

Proverbs 16:22.

> "Understanding is like a fountain which gives life to those who use it, but foolishness brings punishment to fools."

February 23rd, 2021

"Don't let someone who did you wrong make you think there's something wrong with you. Don't devalue yourself because they didn't value you. Know your worth even if they don't."
~ M. A. ~

Dear Diary,

I spoke to a particular person this morning. That was the talk I needed. When I tell you those tears kept falling, they did. I am so much better though. Tomorrow is Xavier's birthday. I am going to write him a letter. I did write a letter; I'm going to give it to him tomorrow. I will not say happy birthday.

~ R.E.O. ~

February 24th, 2021

"There isn't enough room in your mind for both worry and faith. You just decide which one will live there."   ~ M. A. ~

Dear Diary,

   Today is Xavier's birthday. I did not say happy birthday to him because I could not allow him to treat me like this. I want him, but I don't want to deal with him. If he wants me, he can't just apologize. He has to show me his actions speak louder than his words. If he wants to get back to me, he needs to show it. This is what I want. If he is not willing to do these things, he is not worth the trouble. Part of me feels like I shouldn't have to tell him these things. But I do need a new beginning. That is what I want. I will not chase nor sleep with him until the entire list is complete.

                                                    ~ R.E.O. ~

Chapter 5: Destruction of a Swan

Dear Diary,

On April 9, 2019, I wrote my first diary entry. Comparing my thought process about two years ago to now shows how far I've come. I am in the Navy, stationed in Virginia Beach and am moved out. I am on my own out in the middle of the ocean fighting for my country, surrounded 24/7 by other shipmates. My heart is broken, I feel angry and upset. I really want to go home. I want to be in Florida right now. I miss my family. I want to crawl into my bed and cry, ultimately; I want to hibernate in my sorrow.

I can't have a moment to myself and I have no privacy whatsoever. It is currently March 7th, and I am honestly trying to figure out how I got here in the first place. What did I do wrong? I did not put all my faith in one man, however; I gave him my trust and he broke my heart into a million pieces.

I found out on February 22nd. That is the day I said I was done. I could not stop crying. My tears were rolling down my cheeks as a river would flow into the seas. I tried to hold it in, but that hurt. Letting it out hurt. I just felt so mad at him. Mad at her. Mad at everyone. I wanted to physically fight and argue. The one thing I can do, is write. Perhaps this is my distraction.

My most trusted person told me to get a distraction. At first, I thought it was a guy. I was wrong. I read the book "The Subtle Art of Not Giving a Fuck" by Mark Manson. He said that happiness comes from completing goals. Having a completely new companion is not going to make me feel good. Not at all. I want the guy that I fell in love with, but he doesn't want me. He lied to me, cheated on me, and never truly committed to me. We had been talking for six months. I fell so hard, but for what?

I was so excited about this deployment. This 7-month deployment. I was ready. I got everything I needed hygiene-wise. I spent an awesome two weeks with my family. I came back into town and got things packed and sorted out. I was excited to have someone I trusted, someone I thought was going to be with me. He asked me to move in with him. He was drunk and said he wanted to have a baby with me. We were happy. We went on a date night and took pictures together. We were on a great path, or so I thought. I don't know what happened. I don't know what changed.

I'm upset because I believed the Lord would lead me to happiness. The fact that I didn't look for this guy made me feel he was put in my path. The moment I met him; I was on cloud nine. I felt every feeling all at once. It was beautiful. I saw myself with him and I have never seen myself with anyone before. I instantly fell for him but tried to give it time. I have never wanted to be with someone as much as I wanted to be with him. I wanted him to be mine. I wanted to be his. When I found out what he did. I needed an outlet, so I wrote this poem:

February 25th, 2021

Worthy of two minutes
Was it worth it?
Was I not worth the words?
"I do not want to be with you."
Was I not worth two minutes of your time?
For you to let me down,
Let me know,
Whether it was gentle or harsh.
Was I not worth two minutes?

Did you have to lie?
Did you have to hide?
Did you have to avoid me?
Am I that unapproachable?
Did you have to sneak and do what you did?
With whom you have never
Known, connected, or anything with.
Was I worth the loss?
Was my trust in you worthy of being broken down?
Was my faith in you worthy of being tarnished?

Did you have to hurt me?
Hurt us.
Well!
Was she worth the end of us?
Were THEY worth the end of us?
Why am I always an option for you?
Why do you never choose me?
You chose her,
Her,
And now her.

Why am I never a priority?
Why was I not given a fair chance?

Did I do something wrong?
What was wrong?
Were we wrong?
Was it because of the beginning?

Your ex-girlfriend... who was not worthy.
Not worthy of your energy,
Not worthy of your love,
Not worthy of seeing your value.
Therefore, she broke you down,
You need to realize that I am here now.
Well, I was until February 22.
Let this be a lesson.
She was not worthy of you.
I am.
I was.

Your first fuck up,
If it was just sex.
Was it worth the physical trust that you had broken?
Between you and I,
No other guy or gal is what we discussed,
Agreed upon.
Just you and I.
Now there is only one answer I want to know.
Are you worthy of me?

Do you see me?
See me?
My value,
My beauty,
My heart.
How extraordinary I truly am?
Do you see my scars?
Do my tears mean anything to you?
Or are they like water?
Do they not burn into you like acids?
Do they mean something to you?
Why couldn't I get 2 minutes?

Why were you not worthy of giving me the respect I deserve?

Why are we here?
At this point?
Feelings Rica shading from
A gunshot that you have pierced my heart with.
The only suspect is you.

I never loved someone so much,
Yet, I have never been hurt so much.
Why am I worthy of being hurt?
Being embarrassed?
Being taken for granted.
When I do so much for you.
So much, and all I ask for in return is...
Commitment, Loyalty, love, reassurance.
Was I not worthy of any of these things from you?
Why couldn't I have gotten 2 minutes?

What do I mean to you?
Am I just a front?
Just a front for when you want something real.
But when your hoe tendencies kick in,
Do I get the boot?
My feelings get hurt,
Your dick gets hard.
STD chances are real,
Me getting it from you is real.
Why not just give me two minutes?

Leave me.
Live the way you want to live,
But don't straddle me along.
Ruin your life, not mine.
Is that?
Is this my worth to you?

February 25th, 2021

"Falling in love, heal and mend a wounded soul because it's the only thing that keeps us. Alive, it gets easier if you're in love with someone that loves you the same way you love them."
~ M. A. ~

Dear Diary,

Today was pretty good. I had a good setup. We had damage control, so we went to the repair locker. It was cool, I even saw Xavier. The first time my heart dropped, but the second time I played it cool. He broke me a little bit. I feel like everyone hurts me – my mom, my Nana, my dad, my family. I just can't let other people's choices affect my happiness or my inner peace. I forgave him, yeah, but the damage is done. Jesus forgave people who crucified him to death on a cross. He forgave humanity for their sins, no matter how big or small, if He did that, then I can forgive also.

Whether it takes time or anything else that it takes to forgive, I'll forgive. I forgave Martha, I just do not want to be associated with her. I forgave Max, I just don't and will not be entertained by his words. I need to see the actions with Xavier. I need him to own up and become a man. I want to forgive and I will, but not right now. I had to put my fist down first. I forgave my mom. She has forgiven my dad. He never was the father I wanted, and he never will be, but I accepted him, knowing that I could not have it any other way.

~ R.E.O. ~

February 26th, 2021

"Don't tell people your plans. Show them your results."

~ M. A. ~

Dear Diary,

I came up with a list of things I wanted to happen for me to take Xavier back. He needs to change. Today was good and I did not see him. I am so proud I finished the letter. I need to keep strong in my books. I learned a lot. I was just on the right track. I don't know everything, but at least I have the right idea. I think.

~ R.E.O. ~

February 27th, 2021

"Family isn't always blood. It's the people in your life who want you in theirs. The ones who accept you for who you are. The ones who would do anything to see you smile and who love you no matter what."

~ M. A. ~

February 28th, 2021

"Love is not a temporary feeling or emotion. Emotions and feelings change, sometimes daily. But true unconditional love is everlasting."

> Emotions and feelings change, sometimes daily.

March 1st, 2021

"Sometimes it takes a heartbreak to shake us awake and help us see we are with so much more than we're settling for."

~ Mandy Hale ~

Dear Diary, I wrote to Xavier...

Dear Xavier,

I don't understand why you won't choose me. You never gave me a fair chance. You chose your ex-girlfriend twice. The excuse "I have a girlfriend" didn't last long. Now you're saying we work together. This excuse won't last either. This is my last and final attempt. You said "no," but your eyes said something different. I can't read your mind. You said that you were happy and that scared the shit out of you. I don't know if you are trying to protect your heart by breaking mine or protect mine by breaking yours.

Do you want me to stay? Do you love me? Happiness is a choice. I can't make you do anything you don't want to. There is a road of trust. You dropped the China plate, but we can put it back together. You are more than enough. Don't be a disappointment, panda. You deserve love, compassion, and someone to stick with you through thick and thin. That's me! Your midget. You deserve me. I see you have defense mechanisms.

I'm willing to break them all down one by one. Only if you let me. Only if you commit to me. I can't and won't let you disrespect me, embarrass me, lie to me, or cheat on me; that's unacceptable. Nor will I be friends with someone who treats me like that. That is not being complicated; that is being selfish. Read the book and when you give it back, don't say anything; I will have gotten my answer.

You were honest with me. You didn't care about me, and you don't want to be with me. I apologize for calling you a little bitch. I meant that I want you to grow up, be a man and take the initiative. You have never called me out of my name and that's not something I'm about to start doing either. Even though you suggested it. You said you like feisty women and if I called you a bitch, you would be turned on. You care about me in your own way.

You make sure I'm okay. You give me massages. We take quality showers together. We make love together. You watched girlfriends with me. You make me call my mom because, knowing me, I won't. When I got drunk and threw up in the middle of the street, I remember you piggybacked me to your room. You made sure I was good. I think you got me a bottle of water. You've done a lot. We ate cupcakes together. Your first time and that was my first time.

You break down my boundaries, making me think and act outside of my comfort zone. You just won't commit to me. You make something so simple seem so difficult. Men are more difficult than women. You can easily identify Max's wrongs, Richard's wrongs, and Parker's wrongs, but you act like you can't see yours. That's because it's easier said than done. Plus, you act so nonchalant, like you don't care. I know the tough love I gave you yesterday was very shocking and it may have hurt a bit. Honestly, we will have problems for the rest of our lives. Everybody does, but we pick and choose. So, why not solve each one of them with each other?

~ Midget ~

I gave him the letter in which I had poured out my heart, and he said no. He said no again. I was so distraught, but I knew I would survive.

March 2nd, 2021

"Nothing annoys me more than when someone expects you to be okay with something, knowing that they wouldn't be okay with it if you did it to them."

~ M. A. ~

"Sometimes life takes you in a direction you never saw yourself going, but it turns out to be the best road you have ever taken."

~ Abhishek Tiwari ~

The following day was a catastrophe. I cried all day because that is what I longed to do. I wanted to be in bed all day and just cry. My emotions were everywhere. I was sad, upset, and angry. I wanted to fight. I wanted my Nana. I wanted my friend. I wanted him. Everything that I wanted; I could not have. I didn't want to go back to my division. I did not want to see the same people every day. I no longer wanted to go on this deployment. I was so excited and now I was so heartbroken. I wanted to talk, and I didn't want to talk. I wanted to be with my most trusted friend all day. I was hibernating by myself. I'm over here. I'm over there. I'm everywhere. Why me? Why now?

March 3rd, 2021

"If you are not sure where you stand with someone, then it might be. Time to start walking."

~ M. A. ~

Dear Diary,

I talked to my most trusted friend yesterday and I was a mess. I was all over the place. But I just stayed in the kitchen. I stayed to myself. She said that I was on edge and taking things up a notch. That I have my guard up. I don't know. It feels as though my heart is broken. She says I should find a distraction. I just said OKAY. She suggested I go to the behavioral profiler in medical. She helped with behavioral problems. I am sad, but angry mostly. I want to cry. I was so excited and now I want to go home.

I want to pack my bags and I want to run and hide. But mostly, I want to cry. I know he is going to try and talk to me later. He is a liar, a sneak, and a cheater. I shouldn't want him; he broke my heart. I don't want to, but I do want him. I shouldn't want him, though and I have to deal with this all the time. I don't know why I do want him, but I shouldn't. I should not have gotten invested. He told me no after I poured out my heart and tears to him. I will never take him back. I should not and I will not. I refuse to. He did all of this just to hurt me. Never again. Don't let him read this book either. Don't look his way. Don't cry. Don't be weak. Be strong and courageous.

~ R.E.O. ~

As I look back on these diary entries, I realize a lot. Heartbroken was the only way to describe me at that point in my life.

March 4th, 2021

Dear Diary,

I haven't done a morning entry in a while. But today was my sleep-in day. I am about to take a hot shower. I woke up thinking about it. I don't know what went wrong. I don't know why. Was he using me? Did he just want all of the benefits and no commitment? He hurt me badly. Maybe I should distract myself with the help of someone else who can help me stay focused. The problem is that he didn't see me first. He didn't even know my name. Now he does and he is always sweet when I see him. Perhaps I'm just a mess right now. He never even said why he did this to me.

~ R.E.O. ~

Dear Diary,

I am going to ask him if he has a girlfriend. And if not, does he want to talk to me. He seems like a nice guy and I think he is going to be a great distraction. As for Dylan, I will not let him borrow my things. He gave it to someone else to give to me. He acted like he wasn't responsible for returning it to me personally. Fuck him! He's a little bitch. Max is a walking STD, and as for that little bitch, I absolutely cannot stand him. She got fleas and is a slimy bitch.

I am completely done with all of them. Now I have one week left to go back to my division. I don't know if I'm ready for all this drama. I told Xavier that I loved him. Now he's acting like he doesn't care. He is a dick. I will never forgive him. I know he is going to be begging for me to come back. For now, it's a different dude. I am going to ask him tomorrow, I promise. I have confidence.

~ R.E.O. ~

March 3rd, 2021

I'm done because...

You made me cry more times than I can count.

You won't commit to me.

You won't take the initiative.

You have no integrity.

You don't listen to me.

You don't value my wants and needs.

You are SELFISH.

You are NOT sorry.

You are a sorry excuse of a man.

You disrespected me one too many times.

You embarrassed me 3 times.

You have broken our trust.

You have broken our physical trust.

You are a LIAR!!

You are a CHEATER!

You won't take the time to learn from me.

You won't do anything nice for me.

You need to change.

You criticize me daily. Always commenting on my decisions or personal decisions. For example, the way I dress.

You take no accountability

Everyone has problems, but cheating is different.

Your unfaithfulness can ruin my life with an STD.

Your apologies are never apologies.

You do not want to take action.

You don't value me.

I can't count on you.

You won't sacrifice for me.

Your guilty behavior.

You give me no reassurance.

We don't date or go out together.

You don't care about me.

You don't love me.

You find a way to flip the script.

The girls you've made me suspect you've wanted to be intimate with: A, B, C, D, & E.

You made me feel insecure.

I'm tired of waiting, and nothing happens.

You are too comfortable being disrespectful towards me.

You're not there for me.

You are not romantic enough for me. No lovey-dovey stuff, dates, or activities.

You make me worried.

You want to fuck other people.

You are less.

March 5th, 2021

"You can't hate yourself happy. You can't critique yourself thin. You can't shame yourself worthy. Real change begins with self-love and self-care."

~ Jessica Ortner ~

Dear Diary,

I am almost done cranking. I do not want to go back to my division. I am scared to deal with Xavier, Martha, and Max. I don't want to see Xavier; he broke my heart for no fucking reason. I don't know why. I'm really starting to think he was only using me. I loved him so much. I don't know why. I didn't go looking for him. He found me. What am I supposed to do? At least I got through the day without crying. I have to be strong and courageous. I know he is going to try and crawl right back, but the answer is going to be no. I will never forgive him for this. As much as I want to and know I should.

Lord, why do I and my heart have to be broken so many times? Are you trying to tell me that I am not worthy of love? Are you trying to tell me that I'm not good enough? I want to know why? Why, after everything, can't I get something I wanted? I got a taste, and I saw that as my future. I love Xavier. Why can't he just be with me? Why can't he just love me? Commit to me? Be loyal? Be honest? Have a family with me? Marry me? Why can he not love me?

~ R.E.O. ~

March 6th, 2021

"Let go of what's gone, be grateful for. What remains, look forwards to what's coming."

~ M.A. ~

Dear Diary,

I am surprised. I asked him if he was single. I have been noticing him being so nice. And my trusted friend said I should get a distraction. So, I chose John Doe #2. He is nice. He has been helping me with damage control. I asked him if he was single, he got the message. We talked a lot for a moment. He talked to Pricilla too. She gets around. I am so disgusted with Xavier. He needs a wake-up call. He told Pricilla that I called him a bitch and he is acting like one.

He did do some dumb-ass shit. I am completely done with him. Now he is friends with a dolphin. Well, my brother says he is at peace with him. Bullshit, I am so done with all of them; they are full of shit. I am my own person. I don't need one. I am snapping at everybody. I hope we have service tomorrow. I want to email my family.

~ R.E.O. ~

March 7th, 2021

"Love yourself.

Know your worth.

Accept growth.

Appreciate life.

These things will help you through any situation."

~ M. A. ~

Dear Diary,

Today, I learned about this day in navy history. Women were given their first orders to go to the eastern homes. Wow! Today was pretty good. I woke up early to serve breakfast. It did make me angry; I'm not going to lie; I go back to my division this Friday. I don't know. I'm not ready, but I am tired. At least I am going to be missed. I am so disappointed in Xavier. I want to cry because it hurts. I don't need a distraction. I need a new goal to achieve. This is the best time to write my book. This is the year I complete that. I will check it off my bucket list. I am proud of me for sticking up for myself and not allowing myself to be vulnerable for love. I love so hard and when I fall, I fall hard.

I don't need to kiss anybody's ass to feel validated. I am my own person. Life has hurt me quite a bit, but my heart can either be filled with hate or love. I choose love. Makes me feel lighter, but I'm not going to smile and act like we're cool when we're not. I have grudges, I can hold one forever. I'm not going to lie; it is easier said than done. To let them go. It takes time. I don't know. I am just going to stay to myself.

~ R.E.O. ~

March 8th, 2021

"You should never give up. No matter how hard the situation is, always believe that something beautiful is going to happen."

~ M. A. ~

Dear Diary,

I often lose sight of my purpose. I get tired and upset. I am hurting. But I always lift myself. That is one thing I love about myself. I am so happy CS3 chit got approved. And CMC highly recommended him he's behind. Good for him. He nominated me for FSA of the month. I hope I get it. I am going to knock this week out. I am so excited. I hope I win in March. I am so grateful.

I know I was in a funk, now I feel better. My plan is to work on my qualifications and write my book. I am excited about my book. Today was great, and I know that Puke is sneaky. I got to keep my distance. She is bad news. She told CS3 a mess was mine, and it wasn't. She likes to use people. I have noticed that. I am not trying to have any problems, but she and I are not friends.

~ R.E.O. ~

Dear Diary,

Things are getting better. I finish working in food service this week. I go back to my division. I got an email today that Nana's boyfriend's mom passed away. I knew her, she was nice whenever I met her from time to time. She will be missed dearly. These are the things that they warn us about. Things are going to happen back home. When the situation is more in the immediate family, we will be allowed to go home. We still have to come back, but at least we get to say goodbye.

There are days I wake up and I honestly do want to cry. Today, I woke up thinking about him. Why? Why did he do this to me? To us? I thought it was because I said I didn't want to see him with good intentions at the hotel. Just because I say no or not right now. Are you going to go find someone else? I was thinking about the sweetest thing he said to me. "I don't have to have sex with you to be with you." I paused, and I was like... wow! I remember when I had an insecure moment. I told him I was afraid to lose him.

He said, "Well, I'm not going anywhere." I took a deep breath, and I trusted his words. I trusted him. I believed that I had nothing to worry about. The way he made me feel when we connected. I knew he meant it. At least at that moment, he did. Now he acts so calmly as if he doesn't care. If I'm pouring my heart out to you, how could you not react? How could you not reassure me? Own up to your mistakes! Be a man! Not a little boy and just say, "oh, I feel guilty." That hurts. How could you lie to me for two weeks straight? How could you not tell me the truth?

One thing for certain is that we women have intuition or at least I do. I felt the presence of something that wasn't right. I observed the guilty behavior. I just figured he would come around and tell me what was wrong. Explain to me what happened. I thought he would be honest with me. I have forgiven him for so much. The only thing I wanted was his honesty. The only thing I wanted him to do was to commit to me. He just said no. I had to pick up my pride and say okay. I had to take my broken heart and repair it myself. Do you know how hard that is? Where do I begin? Which piece is sharper than the other? Which piece is going to slice my finger the moment I grab it and try to put it in place?

~ R.E.O. ~

March 9th, 2021

"No matter what you are going through, you are not alone. The light is always with you. You might not see it, but you can trust it."

~ M. A. ~

Dear Diary,

So, deployment happened, and everyone changed colors. I don't trust any of these people. I just know to shake with my right hand and have a stone on my left. Those are words from CS3. He said he doesn't trust anyone. But you can't live like that. That is why I give out trust until you give me a reason not to trust you. Living here on the ship, it never fails that someone is smiling in your face as they are planning to stab you in the back. I know it is not everyone, but it is the big majority.

For example, I do not deal with anybody's bullshit. If you show me your true colors and you are indeed a shitty person, I am not going to smile in your face and pretend that we are friends. Nor will I have any social interaction with you, I'll keep it cordial. I'll respect you. I see you, and you see me, and I'll keep it pushing. I'm not going to give you the satisfaction of knowing you can shit on me. Then, when you realize your mistake, we meet again. Everything is fine and dandy. I stand by that. That is one thing I am stubborn about. If I don't fucking like you, I'm going to let you know very nicely. I have no words to exchange with you. Who the fuck are you? Irrelevant in my book. If you fuck me over once, shame on you. If you do it again, then shame on me.

~Later ~

Dear Diary,

Today I had my mentor session with the chief. I realized a lot. She told me about her first fight. I told her Friday was my last day. Time did fly by. I thought I wasn't ready, but I am. I'm ready and I am not interested in shitty Xavier, Martha, or Max because I am my own person. I don't need a posse or anyone to make me feel validated. All I need is me, myself, and I.

My goal is to face Xavier and not have any words to say to him. He said no, so we are not together and we are not friends. We are nothing. That is the way he has chosen to deal with things. I am perfectly okay with that. He did me wrong. I realized today that I'll be dammed if I allow any man or little boy, in this case, to feel like they got that type of hold over me. Or any trashy fake ass bitch to try to bring me out of character, ever. I will survive this deployment. I'll make some money. I'll boss up. I had a great day today.

~ Raven Ella Ozlyn ~

March 10th, 2021

"My philosophy is: It's none of my business what people say of me and think of me. I am what I am, and I do what I do. I expect nothing and accept everything. And it makes life so much easier."

~ Anthony Hopkins ~

Dear Diary,

I am very excited to say that I am okay. I finish cranking on Friday. I am excited and I am not excited. I am just interested. I'm starting this new chapter in my life. Everything is going to be alright. I have someone I trust and she listens and gives me great advice. She says that we will make it through deployment and we will. I love her SO MUCH. I needed at least one support system and I definitely got one in her. I am feeling great.

~ R.E.O. ~

March 11th, 2021

"It may take time, but things will get better."

~ M. A. ~

March 12th, 2021

"The day she let go of the things that were weighing her down was the day she began to shine the brightest."

~ Katrina Mayer ~

Today is supposed to be my last day cranking. Nobody said anything. I'm asking, "What's going on? It's my last day." Then my LPO tells me that I have to stay down there another 6 days. What the fuck? I did my 90 days, why the fuck do I have to stay down here another week? That makes absolutely no sense. Either someone isn't doing their job or something else. I'm pissed the fuck off. CS1 was like, "it's just six more days." That's not the fucking point! The point is, I did my job and I shouldn't have to wait an extra week because someone else didn't do theirs! I fucking hate shit like that with a passion! I don't want to go back to my division when we are in port. I want to go back now. I want to go back on March 12th because that's the day I finished my 90 days!

They are saying I have to stay down here because I'm not qualified to take over the watch and they are too far into the drill. They are some liars. I fucking hate all of them. I'm so pissed the hell off right now. I did all that work and for what? For them to procrastinate. Plus, my fucking charger is still missing.

Later, I talked to the chief, and he said it was just his call. That sounds more realistic. On the brighter side, today is my friend's birthday. I freaking love her. I am most definitely going to make her my best friend when I get back. HAPPY BIRTHDAY, KAYLA!

"Keep your chin up; things will get better before you know it."

~ M. A. ~

Dear Diary,

I was very pissed earlier. Today was supposed to be my last day cranking, but they told me I had to stay in the food service for six more days. I was pissed off. I did my job. Other than that, everything is pretty good. I am okay. I did finish cranking. It sucks that I have to do another week, but my goal was complete. Now, I am just working on my book.

~ R.E.O. ~

March 13th, 2021

"In case no one told you today, you are stronger than you think, and you are doing great."

~ M. A. ~

March 14th, 2021

"It hurts to let go, but sometimes it hurts more to hold on."

~ M. A. ~

March 15th, 2021

"At the end of the day, tell yourself gently, "I love you; you did the best you could today, and even if you didn't accomplish all you had planned, I love you anyway."

~ M. A. ~

Dear Diary,

My freaking charger is still missing. I realized the things that were missing from my jacket had been returned. One of these girls is going through my rack when I'm not here. I'm pretty sure it's a deck female. I am pissed. I asked GM1 for a berthing meeting. I want to ask Xavier some questions. But I don't want to talk to him. I want to ask him, but I seriously don't want to talk to him. My book is going amazingly and I am so happy. Hopefully, we will pull in soon. Then, I am going to be on duty. Sucks, I know, but we are stuck on the ship. Hopefully, we get liberty.

~ R.E.O. ~

March 16th, 2021

"Wait for the person who will do anything to be your everything."

~ M. A. ~

Dear Diary,

Today was good. I learned a lot. We are pulling in early on the eighteenth. So that's good. I go back to my division. I didn't email him. I spoke to MAC. Things are okay. I just let him know I asked GM1 for a berthing meeting because someone is taking my things. CS3 said, "Don't be a snitch!" I think I'm just covering my back. Being by myself is better. I had a mentor session and it was great. I love her.

~ R.E.O. ~

March 18th, 2021

"Life may take you to where you least expected but have faith that you are where you exactly need to be."

~ M. A. ~

March 19th, 2021

"Most people who doubt you doubt you because they can never see themselves doing what you are trying to do."

~ David Goggins~

Dear Diary,

Today was good. I finally got relieved. The new FSA Stanley went down to the chief's mess and I am going back to my division. Yay! Goal completed. I did get angry today. It was so stupid, though. I hate when people in a leadership position act like their marbles are lost. We pulled into Norfolk yesterday and I got five packages. Two of them were care packages. I love Amazon. Working on my book still.

~ R.E.O. ~

March 20th, 2021

"Everything comes to you at the right moment. Be patient. Be grateful."

~ M. A. ~

Dear Diary,

Today I should be happy, but I'm not. I don't know how I feel. I was okay until everything started hitting me one by one. This slimy-ass bitch is coming back. This stupid-ass situation I've got to look at all the time. Right now, I just don't want to deal with it. Then these females that I work with. I'm aggravated. I don't want to deal with any of this. I liked being in S-2. I worked by myself, had a set schedule, did my thing, and called it a night. Now I have to work with all these people.

I'm a little scared. I know confidence is in me. I stand up for myself. There are times when I need a moment to be weak, a moment to be vulnerable; instead of being strong all the time. I hate what I'm going through. I need a secret hiding spot. Somewhere where I can chill. The only place I have is my rack. I'm only there at night. What about during the day? I know hurt people, hurt people and miserable people just want to make other people miserable.

I'm going to get my shit together and not pay these people no mind. I'm not talking to them, especially that slimy bitch Martha. It already started. Earl approached me today and said he heard that I don't like someone in the division. I don't know where he got that from, but I asked him to not instigate things like that. He apologized and said he didn't mean to, but that's a lie. That is exactly what he meant to do. I am not even cool with him like that for him to approach me in that manner. I took a deep breath and talked it down.

~ Later that day ~

Dear Diary,

Today was a little bumpy. I finished cranking. Which was nice. I went back to my division. Then, things took a turn. Martha came back. Before that happened, this guy was trying to stir up trouble. My rack mate got moved. She might be getting kicked off the ship. Too bad, I hope she sorts things out. I was mostly upset about that special person. I wanted to talk to him. I just want closure. What changed? What did I do to deserve this pain he has caused me? I need to know. I'm going to talk to him tomorrow. I feel like they just want drama between this slimy bitch and me. I am not going to give it to them. I also know she feels as if she has something over me. I am better than all of them. I am going to do better. None of them is worth it.

In the past, I have heard about these all-hands working parties. Those aren't a joke. My arms and muscles were so sore from just passing all the inventory and helping load it onto the ship. I did around five hours already. They don't go by quickly either. They last for two hours or more. I like the working party in a way. It's cold outside and it's a bit uncomfortable, but it keeps my mind busy. I get to listen to music and just waste some time.

~ R.E.O. ~

March 21st, 2021

"With everything that has happened to you, you can either feel sorry for yourself or treat what has happened as a gift. Everything is either an opportunity to grow or an obstacle to keep you from growing. You get to choose."

~ Wayne Dyer ~

March 22nd, 2021

"Focus on your strength, not your weakness. Focus on your character, not your reputation. Focus on your blessings, not your misfortunes."

~ Ray T. Bennett ~

Dear Diary,

Today started out as a rough day, but I am glad I toughened up and got through it. I was hurt by the words that he said to me yesterday. I was trying to process everything. Then, I woke up and was like, I want to go home. I don't want to work with these people. I don't want to see these people. I just literally did not want to be here. I felt like I had a panic attack. I went to combat and I cried, loudly too. I have all this built-up pain and, in a sense, nobody cares. I wanted to leave. I missed quarters.

I was in combat talking to chaps, then I spoke to him later, around 1500. I was in the lounge talking to GM1. I had no idea we were kind of in the same boat. Suddenly, Martha enters. I just don't want to be around her. I hate this person's face, her voice, her energy. I talked to my most trusted person later. There was some tough love that was given. She told me I needed to get myself together. She said she was in a similar situation. I hung my coveralls up for 2 hours while I took a nap. I wake up and my belt is missing.

I asked my other rack mates where the one other of them was because she took my belt. They said, "Online, I don't think she would steal your belt." In my mind, I'm like, "bitch is you her? No, you're not!" They offered to contact her while she was on watch and lo and behold, this girl has my belt. As I said, I am starting to dislike these people with a passion. I need to write a poem called, *the words you said to me.* How could I ever forget? I paid my debt today; I am on my way to a 700-something credit score.

~ R.E.O. ~

March 23rd, 2021

"You have to fight through some bad days to earn the best days of your life."

~ M. A.~

Dear Diary,

Today was better. I did not cry. I had an "oh, I'm about to cry" session. He is dead to me. The shit he said to me was hurtful. I don't even think I can forgive him. I know I can, but I don't want to right now. He tried to destroy me. I need to write that poem ASAP. Today is supposed to be beer on the pier.

Instead, I wanted a nice soda and potato chips in my rack. Might be nice to have a movie night by myself. I'm watching the *House Bunny* and I'm working on my book.

Things are getting better. I am listening to those motivational speeches I downloaded. I would rather not go to beer on the pier because one, it's cold outside and two, I don't want to be around those people. I also don't drink beer. I am more comfortable in my own company for the time being. My heart is still being repaired. It's like under construction. My mind isn't right in this instance. I feel like the world is against me and I'm carrying all this weight on my back. Last night I also thought I was about to watch *Soul Plane* with Kevin Hart. I was shocked because I was watching *Soul Train*. I couldn't do anything but laugh at myself.

~ R.E.O. ~

March 24th, 2021

"Stay positive and happy. Work hard and don't give up hope. Be open to criticism and keep learning. Surround yourself with happy, warm, and genuine people."
~ Tena Desae ~

Dear Diary,

Today was a good day. Anything that gets me to work by myself is amazing. I got some yummy opportunities, that's all I am going to say for now. I was on watch at the ECP, just making sure nobody ran away from the ship. I told QM1 that I wanted to be the watch Bill coordinator and I also asked FCC if I could be on the heritage committee. I took my LPOs advice. Goals! I chatted with a lot of people today. It was good. I did like two working parties today. My divo was there; she is amazing. I love her. I got some things that I ordered from Amazon like the *Twist Me* trilogy, my yoga towels and my fucking charger came. I love Amazon. I'm excited. I will cut a bitch if my shit goes missing again. I talked to my mentor; it is always a blessing. Things are getting better. Much love.

I don't think I can ever get back with this person because I need us to connect spiritually. He needs to connect with my soul before we connect physically. The fact that he is not a Christian bothers me a lot. There is something powerful about a man who can pray with his woman and has a deep connection with his Heavenly Father. Yes, to a certain extent, he did respect my religion. This go-around, I'm not settling for less. I want a man who turns to God when things get tough, not other women. I'm sorry, not sorry, he is just less. The hurtful words he said to me. The script he tried to flip. The guilty behavior and the carefree attitude. I'm not kissing anybody's ass. I am nobody's second option; I am the only option. If that doesn't sit right in your vocabulary, then so be it! ~ R.E.O. ~

March 25th, 2021

"Don't give up because of one bad chapter in your life. Keep going; your story doesn't end here."

~ M. A. ~

March 27th, 2021

"Things sometimes get worse before they get better."

~ M. A. ~

March 28th, 2021

"Relationships are stronger when you're best friends first, and a couple second."

~ M. A. ~

March 30th, 2021

"If you can't fly, then run. If you can't run, then walk. If you can't walk, then crawl. But whatever you do, you have to keep moving forward."

~ Martin Luther King Jr. ~

March 31st, 2021

"If you love someone, showing them is better than telling them. If you stop loving someone, telling them is better than showing them."

~ Karen Salmansohn ~

Dear Diary,

<u>What do I do?</u>

What do I do?

What am I supposed to do?

When do you care?

And I am drowning in love with someone,

And they hurt me,

What do I do?

It's brand new,

And they seem to be making this a habit,

What do I do?

April 1st, 2021

"Once you've decided to move on, don't look back. You will never find your future in the rear-view mirror."

~ M. A. ~

April 2nd, 2021

"If you want it, work for it."

~ M. A. ~

April 3rd, 2021

"Believe in new possibilities."

~ M. A. ~

April 4th, 2021

"To love is nothing. To be loved is something. But to be loved by the person you love is everything."

~ M. A. ~

April 5th, 2021

"Whatever comes, let it come, what stays, let it stay. What goes, let it go."

~ Papaji ~

April 6th, 2021

"Commitment means staying loyal to what you said you were going to do long after the mood you said it has left you."

~ M. A. ~

April 7th, 2021

"Think positive, be positive and positive things will happen."

~ M.A. ~

April 8th, 2021

"Life is an exercise in living with the certainty of uncertainty."

~ Jason Kilar ~

April 9th, 2021

"Loyalty is what makes us trust. Trust is what makes us stay. Staying is what makes us love, and love is what gives us hope."

~ Glenn Van Dekken ~

April 10th, 2021

"Sometimes, you have to forget what you want to remember what you deserve." ~ M. A. ~

April 11th, 2021

"Ask yourself if what you are doing has any benefit; if not, then let it go."

~ M. A. ~

April 12th, 2021

"Unconditional love is when you would wholeheartedly do anything for someone. You would do it without them even asking. You would do it because you want to because they mean that much to you."

~ M. A. ~

April 13th, 2021

"Sometimes when things are falling apart, they may be falling into place."

~ M. A. ~

April 14th, 2021

"Maybe it's not always about trying to fix something broken. Maybe it's about starting over and creating something better."

~ M.A. ~

April 15th, 2021

"There is nothing more beautiful than when you prove to yourself just how strong you are."

~ M.A. ~

April 17th, 2021

"One step at a time. One day at a time. One hour at a time."

~ M.A. ~

April 18th, 2021

"Remember, no matter what this week brings, you can handle it. Have a great week ahead!"

~ M.A. ~

April 19th, 2021

"It's better to be single with high standards than in a relationship settling for less."

~ M.A. ~

April 20th, 2021

"Beautiful things happen when you distance yourself from negativity."

~ M.A. ~

~Lisbon, Portugal~

April 21st, 2021

"Never forget that walking away from something unhealthy is brave."

~ M.A. ~

April 22nd, 2021

"The 3 Cs in life: choice, chance, change. You must choose to take the chance if you want anything in life to change."

~ M.A. ~

April 23rd, 2021

"You can't rush something you want to last forever."

~ M.A. ~

April 24th, 2021

"Date yourself. Take yourself out to eat. Don't share your popcorn at the movies with anyone. Stroll around an art museum alone. Fall in love with canvases. Fall in love with yourself."
~ M.A. ~

April 25th, 2021

"You can't change the past, but you can change the future."

~ M.A. ~

April 26th, 2021

"Take all the time you need to heal emotionally. Moving on doesn't take a day; it takes lots of little steps to be able to break free of your broken self."

~ Tere Arigo ~

April 27th, 2021

"Someone you haven't even met yet is wondering what it'd be like to know. Someone like you."

~ M.A. ~

April 28th, 2021

"You are doing great. You are stronger than you think. Don't give up."

~ M.A. ~

April 30th, 2021

"You can't fight for a place in someone's life because no matter how hard you try to keep your place, they'll put you where they want to, even if it's not where you should be. "

~ M.A. ~

Chapter 6: Self-Love is the Key

May 1st, 2021

"Never let anyone – any person or any force dampen – dim or diminish your light."

~ John Lewis ~

May 3rd, 2021

"Discipline your mind to think positively. Discipline your mind to see the good in every situation and look on the best side of every event."

~ Roy T. Bennett ~

May 12th, 2021

Dear Diary,

Going Through Your Through

Letting go is hard.

It is a trust fall.

Involved knowing things are devastating now,

But will not last forever.

Followed by terrible days,

Average days,

Better days,

Great days,

And downward spiral days.

Feel whatever and however, you need to feel.

Avoid the downward spiral days at all costs.

Those days could end you deeply.

Good days and bad days.

Internal conversations and constant interrogations of:

Why? What happened?

Constant confusion.

Never-ending questions.

Questions that will never be answered.

Be prepared for the rain of tears.

Shower tears.

In bed-soaked pillow puddle.

Listening to a song, those solid raindrops will start to fall.

Memories power the automatic sprinklers.

The needed conversations:

frequently, daily, periodically, weekly, and I wish I knew the other.

Necessary reassurance.

That you didn't lose anything,

They did.

You gained FREEDOM!

Listen and watch ted talks,

prayers, motivational speeches,

TikTok's, friends, and family.

Whomever voice or voices you need to hear.

Clean the ear wax out and listen.

Listen for the words "let them go."

The mind is powerful.

Time is fundamental.

It would be so easy if they suck didn't have to suck.

If the heart didn't have to ache.

If the tears didn't have to fall.

If the loneness didn't have to sink deep into the skin.

Re-flash hours.

Draining days.

Long weeks.

Traumatizing months.

Listening to your head and not your heart,

Because you are a queen with standards.

Ambitions.

A bright future.

Now self-reflection.

You did nothing wrong.

Things happen for a reason.

Nothing is an accident.

Everything played out exactly how it was meant to.

That first kiss,

Caught feelings,

The downfall,

The heartbreak.

And now the through.

May 13th, 2021

Dear Diary,

Things have been getting better. I am working on myself. I am smiling a lot more.

Why did you ruin us?

I know the damage is done.

I know the line of no return has been crossed.

Why do I still love you?

Why do I still care?

Why do I still want you to be mine?

So many why's,

Matched with so many lies.

May 14th, 2021

Dear Diary,

Midget Peace

I'm going to say goodbye,

Because there is a new guy.

A guy who isn't going to make me cry.

Tell me lies.

Cheat on me.

Avoid and leave me.

The words you have left on me.

Took three months.

But I closed them myself.

Not forcefully nor physically.

Naturally,

The sun no longer burns,

The breeze isn't too cold.

Life is refreshing.

And it's even better without you.

~

Emotions are like potions.

People are like bottles.

Ingredients come from life.

May 15th, 2021

Dear Diary,

Must Equals Rainbows

To have a beautiful rainbow:

There must be rain,

The blue sky must turn grey,

Going outside seems impossible.

Flooding, lightning, high winds.

To let someone, go.

They just mess up beyond the point of no return.

Your beautiful face must be drenched in tears.

Your world must go from yellow sunshine to midnight black.

Long nights, painful memories, and built-up anxiety.

Rainbows are pretty.

Life without that person hurting you no longer is beautiful.

May 18th, 2021

Dear Diary,

Today was great. It was my first time out and about in Rota, Spain. I went out with my friends Q, M, & S. I went to the Nex and I got a perm. I even bought a stuffed bull and named him Fernando. I met up with some other friends C and S, in addition to some marines. I just enjoyed myself.

~ R.E.O. ~

~Rota, Spain~

May 21st, 2021

Dear Diary,

I gave my mentor a happy birthday gift. She was so pleased. I also was put into three sections so we can see how this works. I am excited.

~ R.E.O. ~

May 27th, 2021

Dear Diary,

Tomorrow, we hit Greece. I am so excited. I had a great watch and twenty days until my birthday. Yay!

~ R.E.O. ~

~Greece~

~Jordan~

When the ship pulled into Jordan, Pricilla broke things off with Xavier to be with Reece. I had already heard about everything, but I knew Xavier would come crawling back to me. I grabbed a zigzag and I went out on the pier to use the Wi-Fi and chill by myself. I sat at a table.

Chief walked past me and asked, "Are you okay?"

I said, "Yes, Chief. I'm fine."

I continued to talk with Nana on the phone. Guess who walks up to my table? Xavier.

Xavier says, "Now, are we good?"

I said, "I am perfectly fine!"

My Nana asked me, "Who is that?"

I said, "Xavier is sitting in front of me asking me if we are good."

My Nana says, "Oh, hell no! Tell him to get the fuck away!"

Xavier then says, "Oh, are you on the phone with your family?" I nodded, telling him, "Yes." Then, he gets up and walks away. I continue my conversation and called my mom afterward. I am supposed to be grabbing food for my new guy, so he texted me. I got up to grab the food. I am waiting in line to grab the food and then Parker walks up to me.

Parker says, "Xavier said that you hurt his feelings. Why don't you listen to what he has to say?" I said, "I have nothing to say to him."

This moment felt so freaking good. I had already decided since this was my birth month, I would like to be joyful all thirty-one days of June. I was not about to subject myself to anything like that. I had already realized that Xavier was toxic to me. After all the healing I was doing by myself, I did not want to give him a second chance. All the warnings and chances I had given Xavier, that ship had sailed. It was never an option. I was the option.

He messed up the best thing that has happened to him in his life. I was never his girlfriend, according to him. We never had anything. I was confused as to what conversation we could have had. I kept thinking Xavier needed to have a conversation with himself, so I wrote this poem with most of the words Xavier said to me.

A Conversation with Yourself

Xavier: "I want to be with my girlfriend."

Xavier: "I want to be with Sarah."

Xavier: "No, I don't like you."

Xavier: "You were just something for that moment. Someone I could get with."

Xavier: "The girl I went back home to sleep with was my best."

Xavier: "I can't be with you because we work together."

Xavier: "I can't be with you because I'm about to leave."

Xavier: "Why are you getting mad? I never said we were a thing."

Xavier: "I never said you were my girlfriend."

Xavier: "I was never going to commit to you. I was just going to be with you until I left."

Xavier: "We are not alike. We have nothing in common. "

Xavier: "You can love me, but I cannot love you."

Xavier: "I love Sarah!"

Xavier: "I don't believe you."

Xavier: "I lost all respect for you."

Xavier: "I can never be with you."

Ozlyn: "I don't want to let you go."

Xavier: "Well, you're going to have to."

Xavier: "I am going to be faithful to Pricilla."

Xavier: "No! You can't hold my hand, hug me, touch me, kiss me.

Xavier: "You think just because I did this to you. I'm going to do this to somebody else.

Ozlyn: "So I had to be the exception."

Ozlyn: "Why couldn't you be honest with me?

Xavier: "Because you were not going to accept it.

Xavier: "Better now than later. It would hurt more later."

Xavier: "I don't want to be with you.

Ozlyn: "I think you do."

Xavier: "No, I don't."

Xavier: "What do you want me to do to get back to you? I gave you a choice."

Ozlyn: "Are you done talking to me?"

Xavier shakes his head yes.

Ozlyn: You're not going to respond to me?

Xavier shakes his head no.

The last four verses were our last conversation. This is how Xavier chose to end things between us. WELL! This is Ozlyn determining the future between us is no more. I knew everything was dead before everything that happened sank deep into my soul. Those hurtful words were the only things that stuck with me. There was a lot more. I was thinking about this poem and everything. Xavier was verbally abusive and emotionally unstable. Two more reasons why I could never be with him again.

> I knew everything was dead before everything that happened sank deep into my soul.

June 1st, 2021

Dear Diary,

I have been great. I am happy I am not sad anymore. Xavier wants to talk to me, and the answer is no. I told my new guy about everything. Honestly, I just don't have anything to say to Xavier.

I should explain how I started talking to my new guy. Xavier said that the new guy asked him if it was okay to hook up with me.

I said, "what?"

Like I had to confirm because that didn't even sound right. I know when I asked Xavier to choose between his girlfriend and me last September, the new guy asked me for my number. He was interested and he was fine then and still is. I didn't entertain him because I was trying to figure things out with Xavier. There are a lot of guys interested in me. I am just the type of girl that deals with one guy at a time. I also don't backtrack. When I'm done. I'm done.

There is no redemption. I told Xavier that multiple times. Xavier and my new guy weren't friends, by the way. The new guy was so fine like he had hood n***a written all over him. OMG! He was short. Lol. But he made up for it in every other way. We were and are friends. I never got the chance to be with him or date him.

When our friendship started, we had an opportunity to date but didn't. I never wanted to let a chance like him pass by again. He was perfectly imperfect.

He had this masculine energy that made me go crazy. He was sweet, caring, genuine, honest, independent, and intelligent. Nobody fucked with him. I just really enjoyed becoming friends with him. The last thing I wanted to do was make him feel like he was a rebound because honestly, he wasn't. He would have been an upgrade. We never got our chance because of life. Who knows, maybe in the future? Just maybe.

~ R.E.O. ~

June 7th, 2021

Dear Diary,

I am counting down the days to my birthday. I can't wait. Only 11 days are left – I am so excited! My guy is keeping a better eye on it than I am. He is so cute.

~ R.E.O. ~

June 10th, 2021

Dear Diary,

Things have been very well. I have nothing to report. I was just working and doing my thing! So excited! Just so, so ready; only seven more days! Next Sunday is my birthday, yay!

~ R.E.O. ~

June 17th, 2021

Dear Diary,

Today is my last entry in this Diary. I am so proud of myself. I said I wanted to keep up with a diary and I have had you for three years now. Today was great. I'm on deployment and counting down the days. Happy birthday to my little brother today. I wish I could be there and celebrate with him because it's Gemini season.

~ R.E.O. ~

June 18th, 2021

"You haven't found true love until you found a Gemini."

"Gemini's: They will always want to have fun with you and go on adventures. They will try to cheer you up with laughter when you are down and never abandon you. They'll talk with you for hours. Yep! That's me! The most reliable friend that any person will have. I keep getting screwed over in the process, though. If I am completely honest with myself, that's how many friends turn out. The only decent ones are my black friends. Every girl that did me wrong as a friend was either white or mixed. That's why I'm slowly learning that I can't help everyone. I wonder why God keeps sending all these lessons into my life. In the end, I will find myself again and again."

~ A Facebook Post I found ~

Dear Diary,

I waited for months to finally use my rose gold diary. This beauty is getting cracked open on my birthday. I am so happy and excited to turn 22 today. Happy birthday/contraction day to me. I love it. So, everything is going well. I know I am still recovering from an incident/situation from someone who shall not be named in this diary. I feel a lot better and I am just living life for myself. I am still on deployment. At least I got my deployment ribbon.

Work is going great. I have no idea why I write less when I'm happy, but I have no one to thank, but God…! He sent me people I needed to build me up: chaps, Chief, mentor and best friend. I have even more friends. My love life is excellent as well. I am dating myself and falling in love all over again. In addition, I am seeing someone, and his name is DJS. He is charming, masculine, and handsome. I can't wait to get to know him better. He is very thoughtful. He is taking things slow and reassures me that he cares about me. He likes me. He is doing everything I had hoped Xavier would do right off the bat. He just surprises me. In one-week things will be different.

I am working on everything that I set out to have completed by the end of deployment. Things are much better than before. I am very grateful. My eval was great. I am trying to heal. I could ask for more, but I won't ask for more. I did this by myself and with Jesus by my side. *I will never leave you nor forsake you.* I trust in those words. He is my light. *I am the head and not the tail.* I've got to ask what's the first food please I'm going to eat when I get home? My answer is Shake Shack. I wanted to go before deployment, instead I went with my best friend to Buffalo Wild Wings, which was great.

Xavier always wants to show up when I am at peace. Just so that he can break my heart, leave me in pieces and play with my feelings so many times. I cannot and I will not allow that, no matter how much I care about him. I am letting things be. I can no longer see a life with him; I can't see a life with my new guy, especially since he makes plans without me. Who knows? Life plays out exactly how it's meant to. If we don't end up together, I hope it's on good terms. He works out every day and he is attractive. I like him a lot. I can't wait to date him. We are making plans for when we get back. We're both going to get our driver's license. I am excited about what's in store for me and to start working on the officer program I want.

Last night I stayed up and talked to my new guy. He waited up for me to get off watch and he enjoyed the last few hours of my birthday with me. He mentioned to me that he cared about me and I was shocked. These are the words I need to hear, not those hurtful ones someone left me with. Everything is great. I really could not have complained. My new guy is a great guy and I am so shocked at how we connected. It's all through conversation, just starting a friendship. I like how he takes ownership and that's just something I haven't seen in anybody else.

I'm excited to get to know him. He said that he was going to take me out in Greece. Other than that, I called my aunties. They are fine. My Nana is great. My birthday was great. Xavier didn't say anything to me on my birthday. I didn't care. I feel like Xavier wanted to talk to me. If he had approached me, it would've shown me that he still cared and what I already thought slightly. But no, he didn't. The same energy he had before, he can keep now. I started dating myself and seeing someone new and better. I'm doing great. I signed up for school in August. I'm so ready! I was just making sure I got things under control and I wished we had an ice cream social tonight.

~ Raven Ella Ozlyn ~

June 20th, 2021

Dear Diary,

I just got off watch. I did some work and now I am in my rack. Today was excellent. We had an ice cream social. I just wish they had cookies 'n' cream instead of chocolate chip ice cream. Watch went by relatively smoothly. Sundays are chill. Brunch is my favorite meal out of the whole week. I don't know how I'm going to be seeing my boo. I am really into getting to know him. He is a beautiful person and focuses on staying out of trouble, which I like. I'm happy and at peace. I know the temptation is there, but I am more than

OK with all these people. I am beyond proud of myself and I am most definitely in love with Ryan.

Happy Father's Day! We celebrated on the ship. Chief has been the best that I've ever had. Did more than my real dad. We made him a card. I helped to set up and pass out cupcakes. They were pastel cupcakes. My dad is in jail right now, I hope he is okay. I love him and especially wish him happiness. He never told me happy birthday when I was little, only when he was forced to. Honestly, I think he doesn't even know my age.

~ R.E.O. ~

June 21st, 2021

Dear Diary,

Today started well, I just got off watch. I did some paperwork in the office, showered and now I am in my rack. I am excited about Greece. My guy is so sweet, he is trying to do something for me, but I don't know what. I want to connect with him. He is so fine. I can't wait. I am back in my rack and ready to go to sleep. I just feel so tired. Later, I got the watch. I'm so excited to spend some time with my guy. He is sweet and pleasant. I wish I didn't think a lot about Xavier, but he is a lesson. So many things I need to know about. I notice he takes many accountabilities, which is a great trait. I like that a lot. I want to go to McDonald's.

~ R.E.O. ~

June 22nd, 2021

Dear Diary,

My days are starting to feel longer. The watch started okay, but Earl made me angry. As soon as he goes to the bridge, he's asking for Max on the headset. I'm like, "What do you need Max for?" He's like, "Does it matter? Just put them on a headset," I'm like, "yes, the fuck it does matter because he was just in combat for two hours, so whatever he had to say to Max; Earl should've said before he went up there. Now that you just went up to the bridge, are you expect me to put Max on the headset? You didn't even ask nicely... this is the type of shit that is making me angry with these people. They act so entitled and expect people to jump and do shit for them. It's not like he didn't just see him. He was just sitting on his ass for the past two hours talking to Max. Earl is gay. He is constantly sucking Max's dick every watch. It's pathetic because he is crying when he's not around Max like a little bitch.

~ R.E.O. ~

July 31st, 2021

"The hardest moments in life are usually the ones that teach you the most valuable lessons."

~ M.A. ~

Chapter 7: The Poison In My Bloodstream

A lot of profanity is used in this chapter. I promised a friend that this book would have the least amount of profanity. I also gave myself this chapter to express my true feelings and be outspoken about the poison fueling my bloodstream.

March 12, 2021

Bullshit

Bullshit is what miserable people are filled with.

They want to pull you down.

Because they are not happy with themselves.

So, therefore, they take it upon themselves.

To spread their shit among others.

Whenever you see them, they are full of bull,

If you let them,

they will shit on you.

I don't tolerate any bull from anyone.

Therefore no one shits on me.

~

I named this chapter because I seem to be put in this filthy spotlight. At the end of everybody's story, I am somehow the bad guy. In my mind, I live with no regrets. I take a mental note of how to handle things next time. The idea for this section came to me on 09-06-21. It was hilarious because the person was super drunk. He only named three people, but he says "there is a top-five" on his shit list. I decided to create my own shit list.

List of People I Despise A.K.A. - My Shit List

#1: Martha "Slimy Bitch."

Martha is number 1. For apparent reasons listed in previous chapters. I never met a terrible person. A person that does not have one nice quality about them. Appearance-wise, I thought she could be a pretty girl, then I used the two extra lenses on my glasses. Martha is super ugly. She looks like the orange-faced oompah-loompahs from Willy Wonka and The Chocolate Factory. She looks like a thirty-five-year-old woman in the face. Girl, you are twenty-something years old. Why do you look so old? I don't have a problem with moles, but hers reminded me of Rubert from *iCarly*. Imagine hair on it as well. She is big and nasty. Smells fishy.

The fact that she sleeps with everyone, I think she is just a waste of ink at this point. She is so irrelevant. Nobody likes her nor wants to be around her, not even her own family. I dislike a spineless person. Suppose you are bold enough to do the vindictive things that you do. Own up to it! Martha is a scary-ass bitch. If she only knew how much she was saved from a good ole fashion ass whooping. I would have broken her fuckin jaw. I know violence isn't the answer, but that bitch needs to be punched in her face. She wants to be a fake ass bully. Then, when she is by herself, she acts sheepish as fuck. The ghetto in me is coming out in this chapter and for that, I apologize in advance. I swear I wanted to mop the floor with this bitch.

I hate the fact that she sits up there and tries to act like she has something on me about Xavier. Let's put her ass on front and center stage. Max does not want her. He has a baby and he is a dead-beat-ass father.

Max is that baby's father because why are you keeping tabs on a baby that is not yours? You are not Facebook friends with the baby mama, but you search her up and go like pictures of the baby on Facebook. How much sense does that make? Plus, you somehow can't manage to respond to the baby momma about getting a DNA test on that same note. Suppose Max knows in his heart that he is not the father, why doesn't he just take the DNA test and let the truth be known? The fact that he is not responding right before deployment will not stop anything. The baby is still going to be there at the end of deployment. He is stupid. She is ridiculous and two stupid motherfuckers belong together, I guess.

Anyhow, Martha looks stupid as fuck telling his baby mama she needs a DNA test. Martha is not wifey, point number one. Point number two, Heather didn't have sex with Martha; she fucked Max. Why are you even getting involved? The main thing is Max never claims Martha! Max probably doesn't want Martha because she keeps having sex with all his friends like Jerry, Fred, and the threesome she had on the ship. Both CS1s, Navy, and marines. Like girl, close your legs; that's why she smells fishy as fuck. You are getting your tactics from Diamond and she is big and nasty as well. I guess that's why Diamond calls Martha her child. She fits the profile.

I feel like I should also bring up the fact that Martha kept trying to talk about getting pregnant with Max after two weeks of sleeping with him. She thought it was funny. In all honesty, she just looked stupid as fuck because if you want to be baby momma number two, that's your business. Do not be surprised when Max up and disappeared because we have discovered that he is a magician so far.

Martha is a broke bitch. She is thinking about everything that Max has. Suppose she didn't learn from those barracks incidents. That is when he is tired. Her ass is going to be on the curb. Then, the bitch doesn't know what two plus two is. She probably thinks it's seven.

Martha, she is so fucking scary. She kept getting my rack mates involved after a while. I wanted to ask them so severely. Did they know Martha was talking to their boyfriends? I am confident that if they did know, they would not be trying so badly to be friends with a slut. Then again, being a slimy bitch is Martha's profession. I guess she gets the point for doing that job right.

I also want to point out that if you have to sleep with anyone to get anything in life, something is not right. Martha and Diamond were opening their stank ass legs for a fucking hotplate; that was disgusting! Martha is like Pricilla 2.0 at this point. Eww! I would not be surprised if Martha had an STD. Pricilla had chlamydia. Martha could have been syphilis. And Diamond could have been gonorrhea. They could have been the best of friends.

#2: Diamond "Stank Porch Monkey."

I never became friends with Diamond. We were always cordial. I had seen her a few times on the ship. Then, I had a couple of incidents where we ended up in the exact location. Stanley, Martha, and I had worked for this homecoming of this ship. Diamond drove her car and met us there. Diamond just helped us find the parking lot. After that, she went on about her business. The other time that I had with Diamond, Martha and I needed to get snacks for an underway. I didn't know Martha had asked Diamond until we ran to her car. It was raining, so I didn't have much time to disagree or anything. All our other ride options fell through, so she was the last resort. Diamond was never my friend. I just stayed quiet. Her car was filthy. Long story short, we went to Walmart and we grabbed some checkers. Diamond gave off the impression that she didn't want to take us, and she was in a hurry. We shopped for like twenty minutes. I grabbed what was close by. I was back on the ship no more than forty minutes later.

Somebody saw us with Diamond and they warned us. They said that it was okay to hang out with her. Just don't pick up any of her habits or reputation. I took that advice seriously and I wanted to know what that was about. I asked some random people who had been on the ship for a while. They told me Diamond had been caught in multiple fan rooms being intimate. She slept with the whole deck department. What grabbed my attention was the first thing people kept saying about her. "Diamond's pussy stank."

My reaction was, "Wow!" That is so specific and how do people know that her vagina stinks? The fact that she keeps giving herself away to the guys on board. Besides her being easy, they kept accepting her offer so she couldn't smell too bad. I found out that Diamond was engaged to one of the undesignated seamen. He did not take her seriously. Every time people would talk bad about Diamond, the guy would joke along if you thought about it. Diamond did have sex with all his friends. For him to still be engaged to her, they either had some special agreement or he was just stupid.

I came to learn a lot about Diamond. I knew she was in trouble and it was best to stay away. However, when she struck OS, I had to work with her, which was a nightmare. Diamond has this stank attitude that does not match her stench. She has a strong body odor and does not smell good at all.

On top of that, she is vulgar, disrespectful, and disgusting. She has the face of a moose. She is always scrunching up her face and making it more dreadful than it already is. Oh my gosh! Out of all the ships, why couldn't she go somewhere else to be the parasite she is?

I am jumping ahead. I went cranking on December 12th, 2020, to replace Martha. Martha went back to the division. During the three months I was cranking, Diamond, another deck female; struck OS and went up to the division. I kept an open mind at first. Diamond and I never had any problems. Then, they put her and me in the same watch group.

We have to communicate through the phones from two different locations. I pass down the information. I'm in my location and Diamond is in another location. I'm relaying the information and Diamond is not responding. I'm repeating myself multiple times. For her to catch an attitude and say, "I heard you." Well, bitch, if you heard me, why aren't you communicating that? Say "copy," "okay," and "got it." Something to acknowledge that my messages are being passed. It was the dumbest shit ever. I could not believe someone could be that incompetent to make something like that an issue. Diamond came from being an undesignated seaman to being an operation specialist. You can't tell because she went from being a shit bag in one department to being a shit bag in a different department.

Then, issues with Diamond prevailed. I communicated with my watch sup. He didn't do anything. He said he was not changing our rotation. I told him that maybe someone else could deal with her stankass attitude. I don't have to and I don't want to. She is super annoying. She kept doing it. I asked to work with someone else and he shot me down. I had to go to my LPO because the situation with Diamond could not be reconciled with me. I thought they said no wild animals on board or pets. Why did they let her on board? I was more than willing to go to war with her. She was as nasty as they came. She was ugly, stank and just nasty. The best word for Diamond is Eww!

Diamond and I never really had an issue. It was never the fact that I did not like her. I just did not like her behavior. She is ridiculous. She tries to cause problems where they don't need to be. Everything was petty. Things got worse when Diamond tended to do this thing. She doesn't know anything, but she likes to put up this front as if she is working on something. We pulled into Bahrain. I was up all night on watch. Then, I had sea and anchor. I didn't eat breakfast. When we pulled in, I was going to eat brunch. Diamond comes up to me, "When you're done, we need you in the Ops office." It wasn't what she said, it was how she said it. I wanted to cuss her ass out right then and there. I finish and I go to the ops office. She is sitting in front of the computer when I need to use it. She acts like she knows what she is doing when she doesn't.

I just started asking the people she asked for instructions. She got mad. I moved to the other chair. Then, she says, "I'm about to start punching people in the face." Bitch who? Martha sitting behind us sound like a damn parrot. "Oh, I'm about to start punching people in the face too," It took so much power in me to not go the fuck off on these bitches. You threatening to put your hands on me is something I don't take lightly. Bitch, the moment you do, all hell is going to break loose. I'm going to be on your ass like white on rice.

I let my chain of command know about it. It continued, so I vocalized it. Suppose anyone tries to hit me. I am going to defend myself. Here is my theory. These bitches are out of line twenty-four seven. The moment I do something, you will hold me to the severest punishment. Which is sending me to captains' mass to lose pay and rank. At the end of every situation/day, I'm supposed to be okay with that; I think the fuck not! There was more. This was the start of a cold war!

#3: George "The Coward."

George is the type of guy that when a female approaches him, he gets big and evil; but when a male is in his face, he tries to de-escalate the situation. He asked this girl where her friend was and he called her a bitch. The girl was like, "my friend will not be talking to you, especially since you called her a bitch." He got big and bold, all up in this girl's face like he was about to put his hands on her. He was calling her every name in the book. You would think he would have that same energy towards a male. Wrong!

For example, we were going to watch and George asked whether he could go eat. A first-class was like, "Okay, just stop everything so George can go eat. It's not like he got the watch or anything. Right?"

George said, "You're worried about something that is none of your concern."

The first class turned around and said, "What the fuck did you just say to me?"

I promise you, George folded up so quickly.

He said, "Nah, man. It ain't even that serious."

Where was all the energy? He was more than willing to put his hands on a female. I swear he was a young lady-man—just a pathetic coward. The next chapter features more of his cowardice.

#4: Parker "The Hypocrite."

I didn't mention the situation between Parker and me. I wasn't going to, but he is the most relevant to telling the story. I mentioned that Parker was my friend, or I thought he was. We were such good friends that he started calling me his little sister. So, I tagged along and started calling him my little brother. When Xavier did the things he did by trying to be with Priscilla, Parker was mad about it; but at the same time, he made it very clear that he was Xavier's friend and not mine. He told our Chief that I threatened to punch Xavier in the face. This was true and I can't get too mad. I just personally felt like he should have said the whole story.

Like, Xavier was trying to get Priscilla to fight me. I asked for the *Switch* back. Xavier said he was going to give it to me. Then, he didn't. So, of course, naturally, I felt like I should have at least punched him in his shit. That is exactly what I said and I'm not going to lie about it. It was a cause-and-effect situation and Parker went out of his way to tell our Chief that I'm just out here putting my hands on people for no reason.

In conclusion, I did not put my hands on Xavier. If Parker was so concerned, he should have stayed in the room and made sure I didn't, especially since he was supposed to be my big brother. When I confronted Parker, he dismissed it and said he could have lost his Naval career bullshit. He said that Chief laughed it off. So, I ain't got nothing to worry about. He also said, "We are in the Navy, you can't just go around putting your hands on people."

So, I took it with a grain of salt. I ain't say nothing to Parker. I didn't even bring it up anymore. I concluded that he was not my friend. I don't care if Chief laughed it off or not. I did not think it was funny. Okay, Parker, you are right. We are in the Navy, and we can't just go around putting our hands-on people." So, I took ten steps back away from everybody. It will be revealed later why this name suits him.

#5: Deborah "Stupid Bitch."

Deborah was my friend, and it is revealed later why the stupid bitch and I stopped being friends.

#6: Fred "The Groupie."

Fred is number 6 on my Shit List most definitely. I already explained his attitude. He is a groupie, that is the only way he can fit in. He never has an opinion of his own. When he came to the ship, I already knew that he had eyes for Martha. It was none of my business, so I never said anything about it. Besides, he was upset that Stanley's wife came into town. They could no longer hang out like before. He started hanging out with another shipmate at the barracks.

Besides PF Chang, the last time I intended to be around Fred was on holiday leave. Fred asked Xavier to give him a ride to the airport. I was also headed to the airport. We were heading out as soon as we got off work. Fred said he needed to grab some stuff from the barracks. Xavier said, "Cool, just hurry up!" We go to the barracks and grabbed Xavier's stuff. He is ready to head out. I asked him, "What about Fred? Aren't you going to call and see what's up with him?" Xavier calls Fred. Fred was going out for sushi with one of our shipmates. He said he would just find his way to the airport. Xavier said, "Well, don't you think you should have called and told me that? I've been sitting here waiting for you because you asked for a ride." Fred said, "My fault, you're right. My bad, I should have told you, but I appreciate it."

In addition to that incident, the only other time I interacted with Fred was before deployment. The day before, we had to go to the hotel to quarantine for a week. I was hanging out with Kayla. We were planning to meet up with her friends from the honor guard at Buffalo Wild Wings. I went to the ship to bring Richard the McDonald's that his wife got him. When I went to the op's office, I called the gym. Xavier asked me to grab him some collar devices.

I said, "Okay."

Before I even called the gym, Fred asked me to get him some food.

I said that I would, also mentioning that I came with somebody. That's not my car. I can't just volunteer her time and stuff. I said, "You got to ask Kayla. She's driving."

Fred said, "Yeah, okay. Well, can you ask her?"

I said, "Why can't you ask her?"

He said, "I think she's going to say no."

I said, "Well, then you ain't gone get no food.

Just ask her. She can either say yes or no."

I make the phone call to the gym. When I hung up with Xavier, Fred asked for her phone number to call Kayla.

She said, "Yea, she would, but she is not going off base back to McDonald's."

Fred then asked for Subway.

Kayla said, "No, she is not getting out of her car to walk into Subway to order him food. She didn't even get out of the vehicle for her husband.

Fred responded, "Yea, you are right. I'll just take some Wendy's."

I get in the car and we headed to Wendy's and the supermarket to get Xavier some collar devices.

Kayla asked the question, "why Fred didn't just ask her the first time they were on the phone together?

I asked what she meant.

She stated, "Fred answered Richard's phone before we got to the pier. We could have stopped at Wendy's on the way and grabbed him food."

I got mad because he acted like he didn't know who I came with when I went there. Like he was shocked to see me on the ship on my off day. I told her what happened and what he said.

She said, "the last time she bought Fred food, he didn't pay her back. He has been acting fake a lot of times. He wanted me to call because he knew their prior situation.

Fred is beyond fake. So, this was our last incident—me bringing him food back to the ship. So, tell me why Fred joined the group of people who spoke nothing but the worst about me on the boat. He started flirting, kissing, and trying to get into Martha's dirty panties on the ship. To top everything off with Fred, he spoke ill about me with the others. The last damaging thing Fred did is in the final chapter. Fred was never my friend. He just played a role to fit in. Once I was talked down on, he just joined the group. Nothing wrong ever happened between us besides the disgusting comment about me.

The guys never wanted Fred to tag along with us. Not to the barracks, not to PF Chang. Not anywhere. Everybody was partnered up. It would have been weird, him being at the barracks. He knew he was just tagging along. That's the real reason he wanted to pay for everyone's food at PF Chang.

When he needed a ride to the airport, I was the one who reminded Xavier not to forget the plans he had made with Fred. I had his back. I took the initiative and when he asked for help, I helped where I could. I just stopped lending a hand when it became apparent that Fred would never do the same for me.

#7: Pricilla "Ugly Parasite."

Honestly, I will use my friend's quote on this one. "I don't talk to parasites." At the beginning of deployment, we weren't even a month in and she had slept with four people on the ship. It was a rumor that she had chlamydia. I believed it. I remember she kept claiming to go to dental for a whole week straight. Now, correct me if I'm wrong, but I don't know anybody that keeps getting their teeth cleaned every day. Then, she got caught with her head between a marine's legs on the ship at 3 in the morning. She was just a dirty broad.

It's not that I didn't like her or anything like that. I knew she could never and would never be in comparison to me. She didn't take anything away from me because I broke things off with Xavier.

It was the fact that she kept trying to insinuate that she wanted to fight me. If she wanted to, she would have. I don't start problems, I finish them. I'm not going to allow no dick-sucking dusty bitch to knock me down. She doesn't have any rank, so she doesn't care. She has no self-respect. No respect for anybody. She was always getting in trouble. Why would I waste my time? Deep down, she wanted to be my friend because she was constantly staring at me. She asked me to do her hair. She complimented me so many times. I was never her friend and I knew we could never be friends. Way before the situation with Xavier, I told my best friend that everybody didn't like her for some weird reason.

I was like, "I'm going to try and keep it cordial." Well, I did. I never shared anything personal with her. I never hung out with her off the ship. I never gave her the impression that we were friends because we were never friends. I also don't like females that put fake sexual assault cases on people. She put one on four different people, including Xavier. He was supposed to be her boyfriend. Priscilla was just wild, but she ended up with Reece. Kudos to her cause everybody knew she had cooties.

#8: Max "Trifling"

He was trifling. He never shut the hell up. At the beginning of the deployment, I was like, "Okay, he isn't all bad." Then, I started seeing how he moved. I already mentioned how he used his friends. I was never friends with Max. We were just cordial. Max is a deadbeat, a liar, and a manipulator like Martha. The big difference is Max got charisma. I don't trust that, not one bit because you know who else had charisma? Hitler! That charisma is how Max had everybody sucking both of his ass cheeks. He tried to use me and he knew I would not be played with.

#9: Stanley.

A big-ass follower and a big-ass bitch. He only spoke to me when he wasn't with the group of want-to-be bullies. Fuck him. His wife was charming, though.

#10: Earl "the shit-starter."

I mentioned Earl in a previous chapter. He also tried to get Diamond to fight my friend. If both had started fighting, he would have been nowhere to be found. They would have both gotten in trouble for what? He was also sucking Max's booty cheeks the whole deployment.

#11: Reece.

It's not that I don't like Reece. It's just at the beginning of deployment, he was calling Pricilla all these names. Verbatim, he said, "Fuck no!" Now it's a different story. Men would say anything to get with the easy girls. Because he asked me to introduce him to a girl I knew. After a while, I guess he just stuck with the leftovers.

#12: Chrissy.

This girl was my rack mate and she was one ugly, stupid, bitch. I never thought she was pretty. She was just inconsiderate. Our rack is in front of the bathroom. This girl would leave the bathroom door open, blasting music at 2 or 3 in the morning with everybody else sleeping. I tried to tell her. Your music is fine; just turn it down and close the door. I don't think she had a brain. The bitch acted like she didn't understand English. Then, I said, "excuse me," and she didn't move. Excuse me is the friendly version for "get the fuck out the way, bitch!" She also got caught in the porta-potty with her supposed boyfriend. Eww, girl. I have never used a porta-potty in my life. If I do, doing anything sexual would be the furthest from my mind. I don't know who told her she was cute, but she wasn't. She was aggravating after a while. Towards the very end, she cleaned up a bit. She was beyond annoying.

#13: Wanda.

I saved the worst for last. This girl was a BM2, and I couldn't stand her. I understand deck females have a bad reputation and they must stick together. The worst type of leader protects their people when they are right and wrong. At the beginning of the deployment, one of the deck females stole my things. I eventually brought it up to BM2. She shot me down, telling me that I should lock my things up. Honestly, don't you think I know that, but we cannot lock up every little thing? Whoever it is, they should just keep their sticky fingers to themselves.

Anyway, I eventually took my charger as a loss. Tell me why what is done in the dark must always come to light. The deck female who was stealing, as I said, did something to BM2. She tried to expose her and the girl was a thief. After the girl who was also my rack mate got kicked off the ship and was facing jail time, BM2 calls herself apologizing. She said to me, "I should have handled things differently, but that female is being dealt with." Girl, if you don't get the fuck out of my face, I was over BM2! When I said something, you dismissed me. But now that the girl had your nudes and was trying to expose you, now you feel like you should have taken care of the female instead of shutting out the people who you insisted come to you for help. Somebody make it make sense because it doesn't.

BM2 did it again later in deployment with Chrissy's ugly ass. She told me I need to be mindful of talking to the seaman because they can take it the wrong way. It was petty and if she heard anything else about it, she would go get MAC.

Well, if it's petty, then why are you going to go grab a chief? Why did we not have this conversation in the berthing? I don't know if she was trying to scare me, but I wasn't. Chrissy was a sloppy bitch. When it's 2 in the morning, she needs to shut the fuck up. I told the first class. BM2 was told she was not to confront anybody else about anything. The first classes would handle it from now on. I don't know who the fuck Wanda thought she was, but she needs to go find Cosmo and play with him.

August 1st, 2021

"It takes a lot of courage to push through hard times. Never give up. Good things are coming your way."

~ M.A. ~

Dear Diary,

Today was pretty much an off day for me. I wasn't focused because I contemplated the conversation with Chief earlier. I had to talk to chaps because I needed to answer the question, "Do I think I'm the issue? If I had to deal with another me, could I deal with another Ozlyn?" My honest answer is "Yes." I think I can deal with ten of me. She responded and said she hadn't talked to me in a while, but I am sassy. I tell it how it is and I don't give a fuck how you feel. That is one hundred percent true. I am sassy. I know that. I acknowledge that not every incident needs a response.

At the same time, you can't act differently when around a particular group of people. Then, when you are by yourself, you want to be cool. No, it would be best if you had that same energy because I know I will. I am by myself twenty-four seven. I don't need a posse or anyone to be in my corner for me to stand on my own two feet. It's like they are poking a bear and then getting mad because it starts to growl. You can't do that. Yes, I brush off a lot of things. I only speak out when it's necessary because in that same aspect, I'm not going to let anyone get comfortable disrespecting me. I will never allow anyone to do that.

They feed off of each other's energy because they are all followers and cowards. I'm willing to look in the mirror and change what needs to change. I'm looking at the big picture. When I first got to the ship, I had the same mentality that I had initially. I had no problems. It's always with the same group of people. I never had a problem with four out of five of them. It all goes back to one person – that demon-ass Martha.

She gets slick out the mouth when she is in their company. When she is alone, she acts like she's scary. She also mentioned that it's like I'm crying wolf. I made the point that I only talked to my Senior twice. The conversation in March and this recent conversation in July. That's a big difference. I only had to speak to him because the work environment was hostile. I know it's like five different people against one. I can't help what they do and why they gang up. I can only control how I respond. So far, I've been trying to voice my issues and concerns because I know if I snap, I'm going to hurt somebody's child, and more importantly, I'm going to hurt myself more by losing my pay and rank.

Another issue is if you let people do what they want to do, there is no issue. Once you call them out for being wrong, now there is a problem because you said something; not the issue itself. It's nothing personal. It's just business. On that same note, I call out any and everybody. I don't discriminate. I play the game fair. If something applies to one, it applies to all. They always like to say I'm just upset about Xavier.

He has been trying to have a conversation with me since June. I've been ignoring the shit out of him since March. I am not about to entertain him. I did have a conversation with him to let him know about Pricilla putting a sexual assault case on him. He didn't even know about it. Just dumb as dumb can be. I am honestly embarrassed to be seen with him. Every time he tries to have a conversation with me, I wonder what happened to his brain cells. This brings me back to my point. The argument they are trying to make is no longer valid because I've moved on.

That being the last day of July, I can honestly say this month wasn't that bad. I got my CPR certification done. Of course, I have to wait for an email and print it. All in all, I passed. So proud. August is my month to get Sailor of the Month. I want that 48-hour duty-free leave chit. I plan on making this the month of empowerment. I am going to get my ESWS. I am going to get a lot of damn quals. This next month is my month and I'm going to be happy the whole way through. We pull into port tomorrow. I'm super excited; even though I know it's hot and all. I'm hoping we can go off base and have a great time.

~Later that day~

This person got mad at me because he had to sit my hour in the spa. He had flight quarters, not including the last time and I took his hour on the bridge. Damn near every time he was at flight quarters, I took his hour on the bridge—the nerve of people. You want people to bend over backwards for you, but when the roles are reversed, you can't do the same. At least hold up your end of the deal. These people are beyond aggravating.

Today is August 1st and it's a great day. I have pretty much been up since 11 AM yesterday. I just got off watch. Then, I was just disgusted. Every time I see Martha. I feel like I'm looking at a parasite. I can't stand her. My facial expression showed it too. I didn't say anything to her because I truly didn't have anything nice to say to her.

I enjoyed the first few leave days with my group of Q, M, & S. We had a blast. The attitudes were there, but we pushed through it.

~

Every morning we have to meet with the division while in port to discuss the day's plan. Max asked me to grab the females from the berthing. I went down there and asked the senior OS where the other females were. She said they should call me. I saw the other three females – Diamond and two other ones when I walked through. So, I went back to the op's office. We have quarters and Martha didn't show up. Diamond tells the whole division, "I woke up all the females except for Martha." I wish I would have heard her ugly ass say that, but of course, she said it when I left the room and one of the females told me.

Just like I have been saying this whole time. I am always the center of the conversation—even at eight o'clock in the morning. The monkey-faced skank needed to get her facts straight because I didn't wake any of the females up once; I saw the majority of them. Point number two, I am not a goddamn alarm clock. You are all grown women. You know what time quarters are. I don't have to wake anybody up. Then, Martha comes into combat with all that damn crust in her face talking about the situation to Max and saying she is about to slap the shit out of somebody.

This is the point where I knew. I just had a target on my back. I didn't even say anything to these people. I haven't even done anything. I showed up to work on time. I was doing my job, but they always found a way to try and start with me. It is always a problem. I walked away. I was upset and I wanted to rip their faces off. I just let it go because I was like bitch do it. I was so ready. I thought this was going to be the day.

Then, I went to cleaning stations. I'm in the berth with a CS. We are about to change the trash bags. I moved the trash, but then I left them because I waited for the bags to be replaced. Diamond went to use the bathroom, not a problem. When I went back to the bathroom to gather the trash bags, the problem was; a used bloody pad was on the floor. It wasn't there a minute ago until Diamond used the bathroom. It pissed me off because Diamond walks around here acting the way she does. She had poor hygiene.

All week long, a female had been leaving their pad behind the trash can, and it must have been her. This one time, she left her bloody panties in front of the bathroom. Diamond did not pick her panties up at all. Another female picked it up at cleaning stations. Diamond is beyond disgusting. Nasty. The guys boost her head up because she's easy and she's putting out. They know she is filthy and that's the sad part. Diamond didn't want to take out the trashes. There were multiple times when after she used the bathroom, the trash needed to be taken out immediately. It smelled up of the bathroom. It was just disgusting.

You know what? The kicker is, Diamond got the nerve to come and say, "it stinks in my living cube." I'm like, "Diamond, you little bitch; we literally <u>must</u> hold our breath around you a lot of times." It was the audacity for me!

August 2nd, 2021

"Control your emotions, or it will control you."

~ M.A. ~

August 3rd, 2021

"Don't stop till you're proud."

~ M.A. ~

August 5th, 2021

"No matter what comes your way, no matter how difficult or unfair, you will do more than simply survive. You will thrive."

~ M.A. ~

August 6th, 2021

"Think about every good thing in your life right now. Free yourself from worrying. Let go of the anxiety, breathe. Stay. Positive, all is well."

~ Germany Kent ~

August 7th, 2021

Dear Diary,

Today was not as exciting as I had hoped. I spent it alone. I did make the most out of it. I bought an iPad and got a breath of fresh air by getting some chicken tenders and fries. Later on I got a smoothie. Finally, I end the night with some McDonald's. I did feel pretty upset earlier. I got the impression that my friends didn't want to hang out with me because I didn't want to come back late. I talked to a few people, then I just told them what I thought. We are cool now. I got 60 days now. It is the final countdown for real. I want to go home. Now my family is going to come up for the homecoming. The guy I'm seeing is also bringing his family. So excited!

~

You know I am getting super tired of the same old shit. These two girls Martha and Diamond are out of line. They want to make these comments of "I'm about to slap her."

I just spoke to a senior. He said, "tomorrow, we are all going to talk about it in the ops office before the underway." I am anxious about it. I think this is the conversation that is needed because I got a lot to say, but I'm going to write it all down. I am not going to go in free balling this time. I know it's all petty. I am beyond tired of it. Tomorrow we are going to squash it hopefully. I know I'm not innocent in any of this. You make these comments towards me every time I see you, I'm going to be ready. The moment you put your hands on me, all hell is going to break loose.

~

"Goodbyes make you think. They make you realize whom you had, what you lost, and what you've taken for granted."

~ M. A. ~

Dear Diary,

My good friend is leaving the ship for a while. I am so sad. I know my friend will be back.

August 8th, 2021

"I don't think people realize how much strength it takes to pull yourself out of a poisonous situation with someone you love deeply. So, if you've done that today or. Any day, I'm proud of you."

> I don't think people realize how much strength it takes to pull yourself out of a poisonous situation…

~ Horacio Jones ~

Dear Diary,

Not this again; I am over Xavier.

~ R.E.O. ~

August 9th, 2021

"One day, you'll be at the place you always wanted to be."

~ M.A. ~

I just got underway and everything is going well. We still don't have a plan or anything. We are just going with the flow. I had plans to stand at a station I had just got qualified in, but one of my shipmates couldn't be found. She was supposed to be on the sea and anchor. Nobody could find her. I was upset, but it all worked out because she ended up standing an hour and a half of my watch. She is a hit or miss. It's like I want to help her and understand where she's coming from, but she makes it super difficult. I knew when I needed my time to get my things together. I understood how that felt. Therefore, I am empathetic toward her. I still have to have a conversation with Senior, Martha, and Diamond tomorrow. Wish me luck!

Senior spoke to Martha and Diamond by himself. He felt a group conversation would be pointless and lead to arguing. I am okay with that. Just like I said, if they touch me, I'm going beat the breaks off their ass.

August 10th, 2021

"Love is made by trust, respect, and caring."

~ M.A. ~

August 11th, 2021

"Don't be afraid to take an unfamiliar path. Sometimes they're the ones that take you to the best places."

~ M.A. ~

August 13th, 2021

"Life goes on whether you choose to move on and take a chance in the unknown. Or stay behind, locked in the past, thinking of what could've been.

~ M.A. ~

August 22nd, 2021

"You've done it before, and you can do it now. See the positive possibilities. Redirect the substantial energy of your frustration and turn it into positive, effective, unstoppable determination."

~ Ralph Marston ~

August 23rd, 2021

"Letting go has never been easy but holding on can be as difficult. Yet strength is measured not by holding on, but by letting go."

~ Len Santos ~

August 24th, 2021

"Be grateful for what you have today; you may not have it tomorrow."

~ M.A. ~

August 25th, 2021

"Sometimes, you have to accept the truth and stop wasting time on the wrong people."

~ M.A. ~

August 26th, 2021

"The best kind of relationship is when they're not only your lover but your best friend too."

~ M.A. ~

Chapter 8: A Fight For Change

Whenever a ship pulls out to sea for more than 90 days, that is classified as a deployment. Upon returning to home port, it is celebrated as homecoming. Families gather on the pier with posters, flowers, cards, hugs, and warm kisses, waiting to see their loved ones. This would be my first homecoming and I was so excited because I had gone through a lot this deployment. I am about to make it to the finish line. God says, "I will never leave you, nor will I forsake you." He didn't. He was there with me the whole time, guiding me the whole time, washing me clear of evil spirits and covering me in the blood of Jesus.

The reason for this book is based on the fact that I went through a lot of trials and tribulations. I kept asking myself the question the whole seven months on deployment. Why do I want to write this book? I want to write this book because it is my outline of many events I had to endure. Every time something happened. I never went back and told people. They may ask: "what happened with this situation?" My answer was always the same. "It was nothing worth sharing." or "it was nothing" from liars and cheaters to adultery and unspeakable acts. Problems kept arising out of nowhere. I never entertained the issues, just kept them bottled inside me. But that left me angry at the world when I think back to all the punches I had to take.

Now, all my buttons are pressed. I have no more patience left for these people. Before I snap and hurt somebody's child let me calm down. More importantly, I would hurt myself more by losing my rank and pay. I will never let anyone defeat me. I worked hard to get to where I am, and I am nowhere near the finish line. I'm writing for my sanity, my dreams, and aspirations. Especially since a pussy, he could never be on my level.

August 28, 2021

Dear Diary,

Today I got up and I did my job as I try to do every day. I went to the op's office. They asked me if I could get something from combat. I headed for the door. Martha was going to ask a seaman, "aren't you going to go get it?" In my mind, I'm like, "girl, shut up. You are not about to do it to yourself, so mind your business." It's not like when it's your duty day; you do it with no problem. Why are you trying to delegate? I grabbed it and came back. Then, Max and Martha were play fighting. Just annoying and in the way. If it's attention, they eat it up. I'm like, "I can't, y'all go play in the hallway or something." But they choose the op's office. It just pissed me off. I'm trying to use the printer they play in front of it. I let it go and went about my day.

I started school today, so I was very excited, and I just put in my headphones to block them out. I tried to do cleaning stations. We were in port, so no one else showed up, especially with this rotation we got going on. Duty section one was supposed to take out the trash, they didn't. I just told GM1 and left it alone. It just amazes me. It's hot. We are all sweating and it stinks. Putting feminine products in the trash doesn't help. The fact that they are putting it behind the trash is disgusting. Then to top it all off, they don't want to take it out is just plain nasty. I know Diamond did it for sure. She is just dirty and I just can't with her. I went back upstairs to combat to work on some school stuff. I finished routing the paperwork needed. Then, I went to sleep to get ready for my watch later. I had shore patrol. Today was going to be a good day.

Fast forward, I am finishing up shore patrol. I'm sitting on the bus to get a ride back to the ship. I'm blasting and jamming to music and my mind starts wandering. I start thinking about how I can try to forgive these people, Xavier mostly. I then started to create a playlist called soul search. I want to free my soul from this feeling that I'm feeling. I'm healing. I want to heal properly. I have been trying for weeks. I keep going back to the drawing board and starting over.

Interrupting my train of thought is the view of OS2 Parker and OSSN George. It is almost midnight. They are both late and they were coming from off base to top things off. We were not given off-base liberty during this visit to Bahrain. It was just them two and shore patrol from my ship. All the other people were from a different ship. It was super obvious, and everyone noticed. I'm just back there pondering and in my own world trying to cope with all the chaos. I have my music blasting and I can hear both of them being loud and rude, yelling things like, "let's go!" "We need to go!"

I still wasn't paying them any attention. I get off the bus and one of the shore patrols is like, look at your OS2s. I respond, "I see an OS2 and an OSSN." They say, "that's a seaman." I respond," sure is," they say," well, he's definitely in trouble he was supposed to be back at 2300. It's 0030 right now." I said, "I don't think they are going to get in trouble. Things like this keep happening in my division and it just keeps getting swept under the rug. Everybody keeps saying something big has to happen for things to change. I don't know what that is."

In my mind, I'm thinking, "I wish it would pass already so change can come. I don't know what it is, but as I am talking to this person, they tell me I have the late camp watch. I'm like, "Okay, so I shouldn't go to sleep until after muster at 0600. I can be up more for the 12-hour shift later at 1600. I go to the berthing, grab my laundry bag, and put it in the washer. I go back to the berthing, grab my notebook, pens, phone, and air pods so I can go start my online classes. I said, "excuse me," as I passed Parker and George to go to the berthing. Parker says something. I look back, and George says, "he's not talking about you, Ozlyn." I didn't say anything. I entered the OPS office.

Less than five minutes later, George and Parker entered the ops office. George opens the door and helps himself to the computer. It was quiet for a second. Then, George goes to Parker and laughs about how drunk he is. He couldn't even log on to the computer. Parker starts blabbering. I didn't realize he was talking to me until he turned around and kept doing a hand gesture with two fingers pointed at me. He's saying, "this bitch is watching me on the bus. This bitch is staring at me and watching me." Then, you go say happy birthday to my kids on Facebook. He is not making any sense and he sounded stupid. Parker said, "you walk past me every day acting like you didn't do anything to me. You told my wife I'm out here doing this, that and the third. You look stupid. I talked to my wife. She said that she doesn't know why you did that."

He mentions Xavier and this guy people thought I was seeing. Calling me stupid and saying I got to work for everything. I said, "I'm glad this is how you feel. You look stupid, and you're not making any sense." I let him go on for about two more minutes. My last words to him were "Parker, you're drunk, you sound stupid and you need to go to sleep." I shift my focus from him to the computer screen.

I notice him standing up and getting closer to me. All the while he is doing this waving hand gesture motion from side to side. He then cocks his hand back and slaps me across the face. He proceeds to grab the right side of my hair with his left hand. He pulls me over to the computer screen. He continues to pull my hair and starts pushing my head towards the left side of my body towards the floor.

When I realized that he was attacking me and I needed to fight back, I was on the floor. This 6 feet something coward is punching me in my head and my face. I start fighting back. Kicking, screaming, and yelling, "Parker, get the fuck off me!" I can only reach his legs and private area. George then grabs him and is pulling Parker, but Parker is pulling my hair. We end up on the other side of the room. Parker pulled out my tracks and some of my hair.

Again, Parker grabbed my hair on the right side and pushed my head down on the left side of my body. I'm fighting him back. I'm screaming for my life. "Parker, get the fuck off of me!" "You stupid bitch!" "Don't you ever fucking touch me!" I get free, and he does it again. Grabs the right side of my hair and pushes my head down the left side of my body.

I am punching, kicking, and screaming. I cried out for help a couple of times. "Help! Help!" George then pulls him off. Sits him in the chair. I get up, and I try to hit him in the face a couple of times. I'm screaming, "don't you ever fucking touch me, you stupid bitch!" George blocks my hits and yells, "Oz, just chill!" I respond, "Nah, fuck that!" I go to the female chief's berthing and I'm knocking frantically. They let me in and asked what happened. I said, "Parker attacked me when I was on the computer." I am trying to comprehend what just happened myself.

They went to get my Senior. A few chiefs were there. A senior OS heard me screaming, so he came to the office and said that he heard me screaming. They first ask George what happened. He says, "we were arguing and then we both went to fighting." That is not what happened. I quickly snapped out of the shocked frame of mind I was in and stood up for myself. I realized that George had already put Parker in his rack. When I started to think about everything that happened, George thought everything was funny until it wasn't. He even tried to downplay the situation and say I should have gone to the LRC (computer room). In addition, to making it sound like it was just a fair mutual fight.

I was very angry. They asked what happened; I explained that he was mad. Even if he's mad, that doesn't give him the right to put his hands on me. Isn't that what he said to me? When I said, "I wanted to punch Xavier in the face," Parker, like the coward he is, went and told our chief that I threatened him. I was mad, and I had my reasons. When I confronted Parker, he played it off and dismissed me. I took it with a grain of salt. He said, "Ozlyn, we're in the navy. You can't just go around hitting people." Parker is a huge hypocrite. He can preach to other people, but when it's his situation, not handle the truth. My only words to Parker were, **"We are in the navy, Parker. You can't just go around hitting people because you're mad."**

Going back to the matter at hand. I go to the food service office and talk to CSCS and OSCS for a minute. My chief just said that he's sorry. That was all he could say to me. I know he feels bad because less than two weeks ago, I brought to his attention the threats they were making. "I'm gonna slap this girl." "I'm gonna punch this girl in the face." I told him, "I do feel like someone is gonna try and put their hands on me." He cut me off and responded, **"Ozlyn, I'm not going to let nobody put their hands on nobody."** The conversation was about Diamond and Martha. I would never have thought Parker would have been the one. Now it all made sense.

Thinking about the training, Parker didn't show up. He did at the end and he said, "this is stupid, and he left." I remember he said it to Max. Max agreed. In another incident, George asked, while he was on watch with me, "Ozlyn, why has everyone got beef with you?" I said, "nobody said anything to me. I ain't got no beef with no one." I asked, "who is everyone?" George ain't say nothing. That's why Diamond and Martha feel like they can team up and be extra nasty. All of them are dirty porch monkeys. Martha is just turning into Diamond 2.0. Eww, nobody wants a stank sardine-smelling monkey. They are nothing but following what I've been saying this whole time.

~

The reasons Parker attacked me:

Reason 1:

He said, "I was watching him on the bus." That's a lie. He went off base and was late. He had already dug a hole for himself and was going to get in trouble anyway. I wasn't the one who had seen the situation for what it was. The first classes and the chiefs were the ones asking for answers. That was his guilt eating at him.

Reason 2:

He said, "she said happy birthday to my kids." Let me break this point down after I explain point number three.

Reason 3:

I did his wife a favor. When we were celebrating his birthday the day before deployment, his wife asked me, "if my husband is doing anything on deployment with a girl, you will let me know, right?" I said, "yea, for sure." He was mad that I told his wife the truth about him trying to get with two of my rack mates and at least two of the LCU girls. He is not mad at me. Rather he is mad at the truth. I didn't even tell her anything specific. What I said verbatim to his wife was, "Everything I heard was hearsay that he did not know for sure." Xavier was the one who told him. Then, it was different incidents with the girls who came up and spoke to me.

Moreover, Parker invited me to be friends with his wife. Just because I blocked him and I'm not friends with him doesn't mean I wasn't friends with his wife. I told her that five months ago when we were in Spain. I do this thing to say happy birthday and congratulations to anyone on my Facebook, so he has been angry this whole time or whenever his wife confronted him about it.

I'm just thinking to myself, "WOW! When you did it to me, it was okay. Now that the shoe is on the other foot, you don't like it." Parker is only mad at the truth. He isn't mad at me. He is mad at the fact that the truth was exposed. It is the truth. When I talked to chaps and said, Parke, told my chief that I threatened Xavier. He said, "well, was it true?" I said, yea. He responded, then perhaps you're not mad at Parker; you're mad at the truth. I became a big girl, and I aired out all my dirty laundry. I had an adult conversation with my chief and chaps. I was scared as hell at how I was going to carry on. But I did. I started from scratch. Not from scratch in a new environment. My soul and heart were restarting.

The day continues and as I'm sitting there with my Senior and he is apologizing, I don't think my Senior let me down. He can't control other people's actions. There was plenty he could have done to not let things get this far. I had conversations with them. I ask, "Can I go call my nana?" I end up being on the phone with my nana and aunties all night. They highly suggest that I go take pictures and give them a callback. I go document everything. I saw my friend and asked her to help me. She gave me some advice on how they could try and flip it. My Senior could get in trouble. I just listened, and I was in the mindset that I would let everything play out. I didn't feel bad for Parker's family. I felt some way knowing that his family would be affected.

I was told at almost 2 in the morning that at 0630, I was going to go and report it. I went to turnover, but MAC asked whether I could come back at 0900. I did. After I gave my report, I went to medical right after. I said I didn't need to see her at 0200 because I didn't feel anything. All the adrenaline was in my system. I couldn't tell what was hurting until I attempted to lay down for those couple of hours.

When I got my examination, it was a rush of pain. My lip was busted and the bottom lip was bleeding. My middle knuckle on my right hand was aching. I had redness on my temples. It was extremely sore, he kept grabbing my hair. When I tried to gel my hair back, it was burning. It had hurt so badly to put a brush on my scalp, let alone touch it. The worst part was my neck. When HMCS touched my neck, it felt like a million nerves ached at once. She said, "you are tense back here." It hurt so badly. Trying to sleep was the worst possible task. Luckily, I have a crown pillow, which I put in between my neck and head. That helped so much.

After the examination, I went to my rack to rest again. I had the roughest sleep. I never had a neck injury before or anything like that. It was the worst pain. When I bent over to take off or put on my shoes, it was so much pressure being put on the sorest part of my body. I guess I forgot to mention that I am on a small ship and news travels fast. My guy got wind of it and he so was mad. My friend was trying to confront him. I just told him to not do anything. I would talk to him when I was ready. I needed time to process everything. I just wanted to talk to MAC and go from there. That's exactly what I did.

I had plans to go help the refugees from 1700 to 0500. I know the incident ruined everything I had planned that night. I was not going to let it dictate my career and my life. In my mind I'm thinking to myself, I'm going to go help a greater cause. I'm still going to look cute and I'm going to go about my day. He's not going to bully me. I told them, "Yes, I still want to go help the refugees." I took my nap. Diamond kept slamming her rack for no reason like a monkey. So, I got up a little earlier than I wanted. I already couldn't sleep that well, so I just started to get dressed and brush my sore scalp. I went to go eat dinner. I keep getting the same responses here. It's either "I'm sorry" or "Are you okay?" It is really on repeat here.

I'm trying to grab food and everything. We had crab legs, so I was excited. I hate that the eyes are a window to the soul. I see it in everyone that they know something or would like to say the same thing. I guess it was too many souls at once. It was easier to not talk about it and leave it alone. I said hi to a couple of people and sat at a mostly empty table. I asked my friend if she could go to the ops office and grab my charger, please. She said yeah. She came back and said Xavier said to ask Marn if I was alright.

Wait a minute, so now you care? Now you want to know how I feel. I just said, oh and I continued to get ready. It was almost 1600 and we were mustering on the boat deck. The day continued and it wasn't that bad. It was just very hot over here in the Middle East. Everyone was sweating badly. Not me because I don't sweat easily, but other people were. Somebody smelled bad and had a bad attitude. He just got here, so I was like, "Okay." The day ended smoothly. Until I got a text sometime later.

23:37 Saturday

Deborah: "Hey, girl."

August 30th, 2021

I got the text at 2337, but I didn't respond until 2024 on Sunday.

Me: "hey, I hope all is well with you and your family. I think you heard about last night already."

Deborah: "can you talk on the phone?"

Me: "I can talk tomorrow. I'm on a 12-hour shift right now."

Deborah: Okay, just give me a call."

Me: "Okay."

Monday 18:57

Me: "Hey, are you free to talk?

Deborah: "Hey, what's up?"

Me: "Can I call you?"

Deborah: "Yeah."

Me: "Is it cool if I call you on Facebook Messenger?"

Deborah: "Yeah, that's fine. What time will you be calling?"

I did call Deborah when I was at the Nex like I had told her I would. We get on the phone and she is playing stupid. Acting like she doesn't know what's going on. I'm not specifying anything. I'm just like your husband put his hands on me. I brought up the conversation we had five months ago.

She said, "well if my husband is messing around, I deserve to know. If you were my friend like you say you are, you would tell me, won't you?"

She was playing so stupid right now, saying, "I confronted him and it's not that hard to put two and two together. What do you want from me? He is my husband. I confronted him and I'm still going to confront him when he gets back."

She says, "Well, I talked to him, and I told him that he should not have put his hands on you and you should not have put your hands on him."

I respond, "your husband is 6 something, and I'm 4'10. You honestly think I'm sitting here trying to pick a fight with him?"

She says, "well, what do you want me to say? I'm over here and I don't know anything. I'm just taking care of the kids. What do you want me to say or do?"

I responded, "I don't need you to say or do anything for me. You asked me for a favor. In actuality, you already knew what was going on. If that's the case... if you are just back home taking care of the kids, why did you want to know so badly? Why did you confront him if that's the case? If you're just home taking care of the kids? If this is your idea of friendship, I don't want it; you can't keep it!"

Deborah asked, "you don't want to be my friend?"

I said, "No." And I hung up the phone.

Deborah wonders why she doesn't have any friends, no job, no schooling, and she's all by herself. I was just blown away. I found it crazy how she was acting like she didn't know what was going on, then she flip-flopped and knew about everything suddenly. If I could have said what I wanted to say, it would not have been pretty. Anyway, the next day I slept in and then I went out on leave.

August 31st, 2021

It's my duty day. I slept in a little. It was 0800 when they asked all the OSs to go upstairs to the OPS office. I didn't know if I was supposed to go. I just walked around the corner. There was CSCS. Thank God! He is always right on time. We have a full-on conversation. She asked me whether I wanted to leave the ship. She asked me, "Do you feel comfortable staying?"

I took a moment and I thought about it. I said, "I don't want to leave because then I'm going to have to start over again. I worked so hard to get to where I am now. I am not going to let them bully me into leaving. I'm not scared of Parker. I just don't want to see him. If I do leave, it would be a new beginning and a less hostile work environment. At the same time, I don't know where I'm going to end up. I can end up on a ship that's about to go on another deployment. No, thank you!

I'm trying to finish this one. It is difficult, but I'm going to make it to that finish line on October 6th. I don't want to leave the ship. I asked whether I could go back cranking at least to the end of deployment. Let things air out and then go back upstairs and try again. I believe I'm trying to heal in a restricted space. I think once I go to a different division, go on leave for two weeks and then go back to my division; things should be better. Let the chips fall where they may in a sense. Give everything a chance to blow over.

On another note, I got hit with another curveball. Parker went to MAC and he claims that I'm still reaching out to his wife. Right after my conversation with Deborah, I blocked her number, but I did not delete the messages. Thank the Lord I did not. This stupid bitch tried to set me up again. Oh, fuck no, ma'am! I got the receipts this time. I did feel some kind of way before, but after this incident, fuck them kids! Fuck Deborah! And Fuck Parker! His career is destroyed. I'm reporting every fucking thing. Including George. Fuck him too!

September 1st, 2021

When I was initially asked, "do you want to stay or go?" I said yes, but I did not want to stay because I would not let these people bully me. My Senior pulled me aside with DivO next to us with an opened door. He said, "you would have to eventually come back to the division and work with Parker and George. You would have to see them every day in addition to dealing with the comments and conversations. Do you want to come back to that?"

I had a mentality of I don't care what they say. That was until I heard one of them. Fred said, "girls, like that they do stuff like that. She probably made the whole thing up." Fred is cranking right now and I have to see him every day and work with him in the future. I promise you; I want to rip that nasty ass mole off his face. How fucking dare he say some shit like that about me? Ole groupie ass piece of shit. He is so worried about trying to get into Martha's stank-ass-period panties. I want to cuss his ugly, wannabe black, old dingy shit-faced asshole self out! He sucks Max's dick twenty-four seven and smiles in his face. Then, behind his back, he is always trying to swim in the flea-infested ass pocketbook pussy of Martha's. That stupid ass accent and vibe he is always trying to give. If I could follow up on the things and feelings that I truly want to do, it would be anything but holy.

Then, I realized that's what they meant. They can't control people's mouths and behaviors. I'm going to have to go back and deal with these people until 2024. I'm going to have to hear and deal with it. Like every day is going to be a battle. Do I want to fight toxic people in a toxic environment? It pains me to say this, but with a toxic chain of command too.

A few months ago, I kept hearing there are two types of chains of command. One that will have your back and let what needs to be taken care of get handled. Then, there is the chain of command that doesn't care and will send you up to the captain's mass just to teach you a lesson. They forgot one. There is the chain of command that will have your back to no extent, where they are hindering the division. They don't realize it, they feel like, "Oh, this doesn't need to be recognized." Then, when things hit the fan, it's like, "Oh, maybe I should have said something then."

I found out that Parker has been going out and getting drunk and coming back and picking fights with people this whole deployment. Almost five other people in the division. Not including myself. Now, I'm like, "Why was this not known? Why are we just finding this out now?" It was swept under the rug. It was also brought up that Parker did this to another female on his last ship. He indeed, is a woman beater.

This brings me to the conclusion that I decided to go to another command only after deployment. I want to finish all the quals I was working on. If I could go somewhere with all my quals and just re-qual instead of starting all over on everything somewhere new; I am okay with the first option.

September 2nd, 2021

Today I went to work with S-2. I was with CS2. We did clean stations and then we hid the rest of the cleaning stations in our space. After lunch, we went and grabbed the breakouts. We just took them out of storage. We did not have to bring them up. When we finished, it was about to be 12. I crawled into my rack to take a nap. I never really dosed off. I was told CS1 wanted to see me in the food service office an hour later. He told me the Captain wanted to talk to me in her cabin when I got there.

It was the conversation I knew was coming. She apologized for the wait it took for me to see her. She said that she hadn't received my statement until today. She read it and said that the situation should not have happened, period. She also mentioned that I had complete and direct access to her. That my safety was her number one concern. She mentioned how some things were not relayed to her, so she wanted to hear directly from me what I wanted to do moving forward.

In summary, I stated that I asked to go to S-2 until the end of deployment. I did intend to stay originally, but I cannot control the comments and behavior of other people. I think the best decision for me is to go to another ship. I would just like to make it home from deployment at least. It would give me time to finish all the projects I was working on.

She said that it was not an issue. I just needed to format a letter of what I wished to do. Chaps would be the one to help me with that. It just was a matter of doing or not doing. I do it now or closer to going home. Because if I sent the letter now, they would most likely fly me off the ship before getting homeport. I agreed and thanked her for seeing me. She is a very elegant and beautiful kind woman. I plan on being in the black history books with her. I will not let her down.

~

Later that day, I'm sitting on the mess decks working on my iPad. George looks around and tries to say, "Ozlyn, I want to know." I said, "don't say anything to me." He left and then he came on the mess decks again. Then, he left. He is a big fucking coward because yesterday I was on the mess decks and there were two guys in there. He didn't try to say anything to me. Now he wants to say something because there is nobody around. I can't stand these spineless pieces of shitbags. He deserves everything that's coming his way. Tomorrow is their captain's mass. He dared to try and confront me.

September 3rd, 2021

Today they both had Captain's Mass. Both were awarded a reduction in pay grade. George was given a 45-day restriction and 45 days of extra duty. Parker got a sixty-day restriction and sixty-day extra duty. In addition, Parker is also getting kicked out of the navy for bad conduct. I do not feel bad for them. They deserve their consequences.

I was relieved that I did not have to go as the witness or victim. I did go to the Nex and get my hair done. The girl at the salon recognized my pulled hair and hairline. She recommended I get individuals to prevent further pulling. I agreed. She told me 85, but when I went to the register, my tab was over 185. I wasn't mad. I just knew I wasn't going to tip her. My hair looked amazing. I had to cancel my hair appointment back home because I had this one.

On the other hand, I'm just thinking that I have to pack my whole locker. All my plans are ruined. I was going to get braces, but I have no idea where I'm going. I could end up anywhere. I am taking a permanent change of station leave.

September 7th, 2021

Today was pretty chill. I enjoyed the day. I got put back to cranking instead of JOD. I was chilling. Now I'm serving. I went to the Nex and enjoyed the relaxation. I came back to the ship with some McDonalds and I started talking to a couple of people that I'm cool with. Martha comes over. She is a lost bitch.

She comes from behind me and stands right in front of me at the table I'm sitting at. She speaks to everyone.

I said, "don't say shit to me."

Martha starts talking about her injured finger. About how she didn't do anything all deployment. The whole time I'm saying, "nobody cares, goodbye, leave." Why the fuck did she come over here?

I wanted to cuss her ass out so badly. You know I don't fucking like you and after all the shit you pulled. You're going to bring your ass over here. If I am minding my own business, why do you feel the need to come over here and bother me? Like what the fuck. I wanted to punch her in her fucking face so badly. Just because you are not around a stank ass diamond, don't mean shit. You still said all this shit. How you were going to put your hands on me. Bitch do it. I am more than ready to mop the floor with her ugly ass. I cannot stand this bitch for shit. She does things repeatedly and then she always tries to play the victim and lie about the shit. A fucking liar and a goddamn manipulator.

September 8th, 2021

I don't think it's wrong for me to ask questions for clarity. I want to know the truth. I hate the fact that he said the same thing Xavier said. "I'm trying to pressure him into a relationship." I'm not. That's not my intention. Going off the words he told me in the past. They keep changing. I was your girlfriend and now we are just talking. I haven't been in a steady relationship in three years. John Doe counts but not really. It was two months. They all keep saying the same thing. "We're just talking." How long is talking supposed to be? I've talked to a guy for 2,3,4,5, and 6 months. That's not a relationship. That's talking.

If talking includes kissing, dating, and being intimate, that's a relationship to me, but they keep naming it talking. So, in other words, I can give you my time, energy, heart, and focus, but I was never in a committed relationship. That means you can do whatever with whomever; you didn't make that commitment to me. That's just like he said, I only said it one time.

Okay, you're giving me the message of: (1) it's "okay" for you to say stuff to me that you don't mean. (2) it's okay for you to say something at the moment and later change your mind without even telling me and (3) it's "okay" for whatever you want. What about what I want? You want to somehow feel like I'm forcing you into it.

I don't want to talk. I'm done talking to people. I have this thing where I'm a people pleaser. I say that everything's okay when it's not. I want and need someone who's going to compromise and not sympathize. I want you to tell me the truth. I have standards and I'm not settling for less. I have learned so much from dealing with Xavier and I am not repeating history. I said that you can enjoy your leave and I will enjoy mine. If you want to date when we get back to homeport, then so be it. I am not about to sit here talking just to sympathize with what you want. I don't have the time nor patience to play games. No, thank you.

> I want and need someone who's going to compromise and not sympathize.

He understood with "well, what I meant…". He tried to correct what he said. It was too late to retract the message he gave me. I had already internalized it and come to terms with it. He and I… are just friends. There is nothing wrong with being friends. We had not crossed the lines of being more than friends. So, it's fine.

September 10th, 2021

Today went smoothly. I was pretty upset that they gave my training position to Diamond. I had a conversation and I'm not up there, so it's not my problem. It just seems like they reward the bad behavior. Diamond is an OS3 verbally threatening a seaman in the division. Saying things like, "I almost slapped the shit out of her." She is very disgusting. They choose to give her more responsibilities. I'm pretty sure this show is going to crumble. Correction: continue to crumble. The great thing is that I won't be there.

I was advised to rethink my decision about staying in Virginia for my safety. What if Parker and Deborah decide that they want to take their anger out on me? They set me up or something, trying to corner me, or the other cowards would try something stupid like that. I just deeply pondered over my safety staying here.

On the other issue about my positions, I can't take it personally because the positions have to be fulfilled. I just feel like I have to pack up my whole life and leave. I was not given the option to stay. My LPO, DIVO, and Senior entertain the value of friendship more. For eight months, they have not had a proper paper trail. They just let these people get comfortable being disrespectful, unprofessional, and worse. They have no boundary line. It is ridiculous.

I am very disappointed. I thought the military was based on order and discipline. Just to come here and experience disrespect, unprofessionalism, and no boundaries, I wish things were a lot better. Things here are beyond toxic and unrepairable. I know it is easier to judge than to form a solution. If I was in charge and had been a part of my chain of command, I would have nipped things in the bud. My department would know that I am about business. I am all those great qualities: supportive, empathetic and an all-around good person.

These last eight months would never have gotten this bad. If I had noticed a pattern within the first two months, they would have been held accountable. Which is worse? One vigilante or an army of vigilantes. They choose the vigilantes over Robin Hood. I understand and take full responsibility that I am not innocent in the least bit. I have my struggles, and I have my moments.

September 13th, 2021

"Never stop being a good person because of bad people!"

~ Unknown ~

Today started badly. I was seasick and I was not doing so well. I had no idea that today was my early day, so, I was an hour late. I came in and I felt bad because I was not as much help. I tried pushing through it and I did a little bit. Anyway, CS1 came and told me CTT1 was looking for me. He was asking me about the long-range training plan. I told him I was working on it. I thought I had a rough sketch on the share drive.

He says, "No, there isn't one."

I said, "oh, okay, well, whomever takes over can just create one.

He says, "you never do a turnover like that."

I said, "I never turned it over. When I got the position, I created everything from scratch. You want my work to be passed on as somebody else's work. Just to say that they did it. Then, at the same time, you are trying to make it seem like it's my fault. As if I wanted to step down or something. It was situational."

He said, "no, I'm just saying anything you do in the navy. You never just leave people to work on it themselves."

He pissed me off because that is exactly what happened. I took over, and I had to do and figure everything out myself. You can just pick a bunch of topics and change them as time passes.

Then he said, "it doesn't work like that."

That is exactly how it works because that was my program and that's exactly what I did. As long as the topic is covered, it doesn't matter when. I went upstairs and I asked to speak to him. Overall, what he said is it's my fault that I'm leaving. I could have thrived here, but I let people get to me. I need tougher skin.

NO! That is not the case at all. I'm not sorry that I did not conform to the division. I am not disrespectful, or unprofessional nor do I act like an untrained monkey. Unlike the people they entertain and act like everything is a big joke. That's why they don't respect our chain of command. It is crazy how 8 months of situations and nothing is documented thus far. Now, they realize that maybe I should have said something or addressed it. Our division is in the spotlight. Maybe it wasn't just pettiness or boys being boys. Now they want to try and act like they are working on things now. I am so glad I'm leaving. I am so glad I don't have to deal with these disgusting people. They are shit.

I took my ESWS board exam and I passed. I failed operations. I failed it on purpose. I had some lookups for supply and navigation. I also failed engineer. I stopped studying more than three weeks ago. I'm about to leave, be on another platform and do my ritual. I wanted to get it. I worked hard for it. Now I have to start over and get it again. At least it's not over. That's all I wanted. I am so proud of myself. As much as I have a lot of thoughts out of anger and frustration, I am a strong person, I know that for sure.

In addition, I understand the advice that I got of reconsidering getting stationed in the same state. I was about to take my board for ESWS. I felt someone staring at me while I was standing outside of the gator chapel. I looked up and it was George. He moved out the light as soon as I looked up. Besides being a coward, he is a huge psycho. The moment a man is in his face, he folds up quickly. But because I'm a female, he wants to antagonize me. Why can't he have that same energy with a man? Because he is a whole woman at heart, a young lady-man, to be specific.

I am not scared of nobody in my division. I would happily go to war with a lot of people. I'm talking fight to the finish. I hate these people so fucking much. I can't even be around them without getting annoyed. It has been a wonderful stress relief not being up there and working with them. I never signed up to join the circus full of monkeys.

September 15th, 2021

Every day is a great day because God woke me up. It is only God willing. I am trying to understand a lot of the emotions that I am feeling. The answer is no answer. The answer is just nowhere to be found. I am just pure angry on the inside. If only I could truly put out my thoughts and my true feelings about a lot of people. Deep down, I know that I can't. I know it's not right. I know it is ungodly. It would only cause me further pain. I have to write a resignation letter for Diamond to be a petty training officer. Lord knows how I truly feel about that porch monkey. I am going to act civilized. I'm going to get it drafted and sign it. I'll give it to her, with no ill will. This is a test from God.

It took me the whole deployment to figure out this question. Why do I keep having issues in my department? Why do I keep bumping heads with everyone? Why? Why? Why? I finally figured out the answer. Today September 15th. Often, the answer is sitting in plain sight, but not mine. Mine was in me. This whole time. It's because of my character, my individualism, my inner peace, my beauty, and my everything.

The answer to my question is simple. Jealousy and envy, of course. I understand now. That I would have never fit in with them and there was nothing I could do to not have the problems that I have had with them. They are beyond jealous of me. Nobody likes either of them. I am a hard worker. I am well respected, and I give respect to others who respect me. I can be a nasty bitch – anyone can, honestly. Me repeatedly never stooping to their level killed them little by little. The fact that I held my own against a six-foot chump says a lot.

Moreover, how about I am always the center of their conversation? I am strong and courageous. I got heart. I am ambitious. I have respect for myself. I have honor, courage, and commitment. I am all the things they wish they could be. After one day of cranking, I was up for sailor of the quarter last quarter. I was chosen to go to the chief's mess. During this deployment, I went from being pushed into a dark black hole to an ascension to my next level of character. Which is even more badass than before. I am more. I am greater. I am history in the making. This is my world. I am going to take it head-on by myself. With me, myself, and I have my own back.

After tonight I won't trouble myself with any of these people. I won't converse, address, or pity any of them. They are irrelevant. They are bottom feeders. I was never meant to intertwine with them. They were never worthy of my kind heart and wonderful spirit. Everyone fears a proud, strong, black, intelligent woman. They hate on me and they don't even know me. They fight demons daily. I let the Lord fight my battles. No weapon formed against me shall prosper. It won't work and it will never work. I wanted revenge so badly. I'm going to pray to God to strike all my enemies down one by one. The best revenge is knowing that God is handling it. I keep getting mad at my chain of command for not acting. God sees all. He is almighty. They will suffer at the hands of the Lord. I am highly favored.

It would hurt even more if I prayed for them. I prayed that they receive everything that was coming their way. I am going to say the same thing I said to Xavier when I first confronted him. I am done! I was done before I even knew I was subconsciously done. I have no idea what the future holds, but I know there is hope. I am going to end this story my way. I will begin my sequel when I'm ready.

September 17th, 2021

Today I took my OS2 advancement test. I wish I knew a lot, but the truth is, I made a lot of educated guesses. Oh, well. What's meant to be is meant to be. I need to get caught up on my homework. At least it is not hard. Something I can do with no problem.

I thought going to S-2 would help me escape my division. Martha and Diamond found their way to fraternization with the first classes down here. It is disgusting. They are creating new lows for themselves. As if their fraternization with our divo wasn't enough. Or the fact that Martha and Diamond had a threesome on the ship in one of the CBR rooms. Diamond had sex in a porta-potty with one of the guys on the ship. Diamond also had sex with Max during this deployment. Yes, Max, as in Martha's boyfriend.

Martha keeps having sex with all of Max's friends. I'm more than certain that she and Fred hooked up. They were already seen kissing and he was massaging her inner thigh while they were on the watch. I could never and would never associate myself with these girls. I have way too much respect for myself. When white girls do stuff like this, I am aware that they get away with it. But, when a black girl does it, she is called every name in the book. Her name is dragged through mud and dirt.

Deployment is about to end. Pretty soon, everybody is going to take off their sea goggles. Then, answer to the question of how many people did you sleep with over deployment? If the number is more than one. That is just nasty. I just cannot come to terms with how they both stink. They smell fishy. They have no self-respect. What's worse is they have no shame.

Later today, I was in the FSO office where the CSS has three computers. After chaps' services, I went in there to do my homework. I was doing pretty good when Diamond was called into the FSO office by one of the CSS. They were very flirtatious. I was uncomfortable. I got even more uncomfortable when one of them reached for her leg. I went to talk to one of the CSS about it. They asked if I wanted to tell Senior I said no. I said, "I'm trying to lay low until I leave. I'm just going to say something." So went back in and it wasn't even five minutes and I asked to speak to them. I asked Diamond to please step out.

I said, "CS1s, I came down here to distance myself from my division. I can see the same things that were happening up top happening again. I was comfortable and now I feel uncomfortable. Perception is reality."

CS1 asked, "what do you mean perception is reality?"

I said, "perception is the reality. That's all I'm going to say."

CS1 said, "I don't know what you both have got going on and I don't care. I talk to you and I talk to her. This is our space; you can't dictate who comes and goes. There are other computers, you just happened to use this one. We are all on the boat together."

I said, "I completely understand CS1." I packed all my things and I left the food service office.

The whole first class is having sex and flirting with a third class. Like, there is no shame. He spoke for both. "They don't care about me and that's their space." I'm trying to stay low until I leave. I will never use the food service office again. I went and talked to Chaps about it. He offered me his computer. He also offered me the computer in the chapel to use with another shipmate as well. I went to Gyro and I asked to use theirs. They said it was okay. I guess I am slowly learning about the real leaders in the navy. Or at least the people's true colors that lead me on this ship.

I guess history keeps repeating itself. I just literally cannot conform to the behaviors of these people. I like work. I like my personal life to be personal. I did shit where I ate in the past. Nobody knew about Xavier and me. We didn't even talk at work, let alone flirt, or do anything to make others uncomfortable or aware of what we had going on. Everybody does not think the same nor have the same common sense.

September 18th, 2021

What would it take for me to be happy at my current job? It would take a clean house. Getting rid of all the bad eggs. Unfortunately, the majority of the eggs are bad. Therefore, I think I should just leave. It is better this way. I will be the edible egg in a new batch of eggs, those are not rotten or smell bad. Or at least not that I am aware of.

In all seriousness, I would love to think I have a great chain of command, but knowing what I now know, I am not so very sure. They choose to reward the bad behavior. Or rather keep the peace. Letting people who are out of line continue to break the rules and disrespect everyone. They love to say, "I'll talk to that person," to make them think that the situation is being handled. Or maybe they are giving out a few consequences. Damn! Eight months of verbal warnings. Are you serious?

I will never be happy here. Not happy or comfortable. Not comfortable knowing that there are no consequences, leaders who are not going to listen, leaders who are not going to act or leaders who are not going to fraternize with their junior sailors. I am beyond disappointed about the first command. I don't plan on being an OS for long. I want to become an officer, maybe then I can be the change toward a better environment. A better future.

I wanted to send my letter today. Takes ten days for me to get orders and everything, so I have to wait until the 25th of September to send it if I want to see homecoming. It sucks. Hopefully, I don't have to be miserable here for too long. The situation that happened last night makes me feel like this is another area where they let Diamond take over. Her wrongs are once again right, according to my so-called leaders. I hate these people.

Today is an ice cream social. I am beyond ready to leave. I was upset about the situation that happened yesterday. I went and had a conversation with the CO. I asked her whether I was supposed to check out with them and have a conversation. She said, "yes." I told her I would like to write her a letter expressing my concerns and the problems I was having. She said she looks forward to reading it and taking it seriously. I also gave her a little insight into what happened in the food service office. She said she would address the situation. I am beyond relieved because I know there is always someone there to listen. And if they don't listen, I'll go talk to someone else.

I was serving. Boy! Do I hate serving these people? It gets so aggravating. People are all doing the same thing, begging for more food. They just came through the line. We have portion sizes for a reason. Very inconsiderate for the next person. Then, when we run out of food, they want to get mad. These people are something else.

I am so ready to punch Martha's ass in the face. She came through the line. I gave her the correct portion size and I put her tray on the counter. Later, she went to say she couldn't go through the line. She comes through the line with Diamond right there. I did the same thing I did at lunch. I sat her tray on the top counter. I don't have to hand it to you. She is so scary. What Diamond gone do. I will beat her ass too. They are such parasites.

September 19th, 2021

I made the wrong decision. I went and spoke to the CO because I did not want to talk to my Senior about the situation. I did not want to and I still ended up having to talk to her anyway. I had a conversation with her and we cleared the air. I feel bad. I also told her what I knew from earlier in deployment. CS1 makes females feel uncomfortable. I wish things were better. I wish I didn't have to deal with these people. I know my division most likely does see me differently. They will reap what they sow.

Chapter 9: Homecoming

September 20th, 2021

Dear Diary, I wrote a letter to CO...

From: OS3 Raven E. Ozlyn, USN

To: CO.

Subject: MY EXPERIENCE IN THE OI DIVISION

1. When I first came on board this platform, I had hoped to excel in the operations department. It is with a heavy heart that I have to depart earlier than December 2024 because of an incident with another OS. After the incident, I initially wanted to stay. Truth is, I did not feel welcomed back to my division. I have been very vocal about the issues. I was given the impression that it was more of a relief that I was leaving. I will have to pack up my whole life and change commands. I was angry at first, but after the events and conversations that followed, I am beyond relieved that I am leaving. If I were to stay and return to my division, which exemplifies a hostile work environment, I would have never been comfortable here for the following reasons.

2. I refuse to stoop to the level of the individuals who are antagonistic and problematic towards other sailors. Senior second-class OSs are asking me to address problems within the division. Newer OSs are slowly learning the divisional setup and arrangement. P's had a rough eight months in Operations. I spoke with my chain of command to make them aware of these circumstances on multiple occasions. It feels as if they heard me but didn't listen. They dismiss it as "pettiness" or "everybody just does not like each other." With everything happening, they are beginning to realize that may not have been the case.

3. The major problem in the OI division is the lack of respect, professionalism, order and above all: discipline. I was content to just leave the platform and hope for better at my new command. I asked to work in S-2 to distance myself from the problems I was facing in OI: only for the problems to follow me downstairs. I have a voice and it deserves to be heard. I cannot help the fact that there is quantity over quality. Few in the division uphold the standards and there are plenty who do not.

4. Instead of addressing the issues or nipping things in the bud, Divisional leadership reprimands the people who speak up and voice the problems and concerns within the division. I was told by my LPO, basically, "if I would have conformed to the way things are, I would have excelled?" I will not apologize for being respectful and professional. I value discipline and I see the value in professional boundaries. I will not apologize for feeling uncomfortable in a hostile work environment. Furthermore, I am not an attention-seeking person. If I ask to speak with a person in private, for whatever reason, whether good or bad, it is none of their business. I cannot control what they choose to assume about the conversation. On that note, it seems like I am being punished for voicing the issues I see in my chain of command. I get the impression (from within the division) that speaking with my chain of command is a problem.

5. Disrespect for others occurs in the open. I am not one to antagonize or be mean to others. Nor will I be okay with making others feel uncomfortable. This is the same treatment the senior OSs are receiving as well. Their attempts to hold people accountable fail because our leadership interferes. It is like a never-ending cycle, with the same outcome every time. The definition of going insane is doing the exact same thing over and over and expecting a different outcome.

6. The message I receive from being in my division is that it is okay to: threaten people; put your hands on people; fraternize with our leaders and break general orders 1, 2, 3, 5, 6, 7, and 11. In the end, there is no accountability. It is "okay" to break articles because there are no repercussions. One specific example: my LPO said, "It's like trying to beat a dead horse." That would be the only way for me to express and pinpoint the topic and situations I am referring to. He also stated, "It was like I was trying to tell him how to do his job."

7. I was not trying to tell him how to do his job. My question was about what consequences came to the second class who slept through all the transits on the geek's station. On one of the transits, our LPO caught him sleeping. He then told the sailor to stand up if he felt sleepy. The second class left CIC, came back five minutes later, returned to his chair, sat down, and went right back to sleep. Ops was TAO at the time, but he was facing the opposite direction. Our LPO did nothing about the situation. This same second class called out a seaman for sleeping on a watch. This was very hypocritical, as that second class suggested that the watch sup have a conversation with our senior about that seaman sleeping on the watch.

8. My senior advised me that "when someone gets in trouble, you are not going to know when someone gets in trouble." However, everyone finds out because: (1) it is always the same people who love being the center of attention. Verbally saying, "No, I never get in trouble," or "Yeah, I just got a counseling chit," or "Yeah, we had a conversation, but it was nothing." (2). When something happens, that is bigger and bolder than the last time. That is when the light is shed over everything that happened in the past, finally exposing everything that was previously swept under the rug.

9. On top of everything, the individuals who are disrespectful and unprofessional are being praised within the division. They are being placed in leadership roles, entertained by the chain of command and by others who have also joined in on their complacency:

Following in their footsteps: creating multiple vigilantes in the division. Positions of leadership should be the result of working hard, doing your job, and being a team player, rather than being a bully, or somehow liked for all the wrong reasons. Such as not listening to the senior OSs or our LPO. But, instead of being friends with our Senior and DivO or being able to kiss up well.

10. As a result of this, our chain of command is giving its power away. They are allowing the problems to take over. They give too many chances, pushing the boundary line further and further back to the point where there are no boundaries. Individuals have voiced that they do not respect our LPO, Senior, or DivO. The comments and rumors they are indulging in are beyond ridiculous. Instead of helping, they are hindering the division. It is really sad and scary when people in the OI division are saying: "they don't trust our chain of command" or that "our division runs on friendship." "Some individuals will never listen and do their jobs, and never face any consequences.", "As long as this person kisses up to our leaders, they are going to continue to get away with the things that they do." In the OI division, you can get away with murder.

11. Over these six months, many verbal conversations have been had. So many incidents have gone undocumented. In the end, many people feel like there is no hope. Their voices are suppressed, and they are more than willing and want to leave. Everyone is aware of the truth, but no one dares to speak up. If there was any integrity to do the right thing, there was never a commitment.

12. Just because one person is acting this way does not make it right. I know it is right that I have morals, respect for others, self-respect, and dignity. On account of that, I do not think I would have ever conformed to the behavior within my division. The situation started to go downhill back in October. Two shipmates were openly malingering, and everyone knew, but they were never held accountable.

13. During my time in OI, I have shown that: I can work hard; I can work on my qualifications: I can be a team player; I can make every underway; I cannot complain; I can be professional; I can be respectful and well respected; I can do a great job. I have taken the initiative and voiced how I desired to learn and take on more responsibility. For the past fifteen months, I have picked up the slack for an OS that never did its job. This same OS never worked on their qualifications, never listened to our senior (going back to when he was chief), continuously stirred up trouble, lied, and played the victim card repeatedly. This left everyone else at their mercy, and they were not held accountable. This sailor regularly displays blatant disrespect and unprofessionalism. I would never call my DivO by their first name. I would never show up an hour late to watch just to have a conversation with a person of the opposite sex. I would never be comfortable enough to go to sleep during a sea and anchor, knowing that our chief requested that every OS be in combat. I would never be comfortable saying, "My name is so and so. I do what I want."

14. It came to the point where I was beyond frustrated with this person, always playing the victim, and trying to throw me under the bus. In the beginning, I thought responding to the incidents would just make things worse. So, I didn't vocalize how I felt at first. Then, this individual started involving others, forming a posse, leaving me to stand by myself. Creating a bullying and hostile environment. At the time of our ROM before deployment, I started addressing and speaking up about how the setup in the division was ridiculous; I find myself being ridiculed for addressing such issues. To top things off, individuals that have struck OS and come up top are only contributing to the division going up in flames.

15. Perhaps if I was like the others who have given up or conformed maybe things would have gone smoother. Maybe I care a little too much. The fact of the matter is I would withstand alone one than compromise my integrity. I plan to make the Navy my career. After my first tour, I want to become a JAG. Even if this is how the Navy is, that does not mean it needs to continue to be this way.

16. Favoritism is visible. I do not feel safe in my own space. On top of being uncomfortable, I verbally mentioned multiple times that it was clear that certain individuals were threatening me and could put their hands on me and not be held accountable. But, if I were to put my hands on them, I would be held accountable to the max. I repeatedly said, "If this person touches me, I'm going to hit them back." They were spoken to and told this type of behavior was unacceptable. Yet, as soon as I was not in the OI division, those same individuals continued to threaten another seaman within the division. Their actions send the message that this is their division, and they run the show.

17. What is truly sad about everything that I went through with these people is I never had an issue with either of them, to begin with, maybe a disagreement or trying to address their behavior, but I had no issue with the rest of the division, except for one person. I made it clear that I had no desire to be their friend: that was it. They seem to need to feed off another person to antagonize people. I see it, and everybody else sees it. I realize nobody is perfect and that nobody is innocent, especially me. I have taken a long and hard look in the mirror. I have dug myself out of a very deep and dark hole, and now I stand tall and strong. I may have some wrong ideas about how the Navy is rather than how it should be. As humans, we can all learn and should improve from our mistakes.

18. I have worked hard for everything that I sought after. I finished my time cranking in the CPO mess. I became an advanced E-4 with E-5 qualifications. I've picked up a collateral duty. I've signed up for USMAP. I am involved in MWR, multicultural, and cruise book committees. I've signed up for college, and I am working towards my bachelor's. I never wanted to be friends with either of these people. I would gladly help every one of them in my division. However, the moment someone talks down on me, they join in, in a heartbeat. I will not condone people who talk bad about me and then smile on my face. I know that a snake never stops being a snake; it just sheds its skin and becomes a bigger snake. I've tried to keep it professional with these people. I've worked hard at being a petty training officer. I worked so hard to get nav scope, only to be able to go to one brief, only to ho step-down and give everything that I've worked hard for to someone else.

19. I am beyond disappointed in my division, LPO, Senior, and DivO. They have let me down, and I let them down. I am a strong person. I know this command just wasn't meant for me. Because what's meant to be, will be. I kept holding on to a place that was not on the maturity level that I was on. When I first came to the ship, it was not like this. The OI had some orders. Our LPO at the time left this platform an OS1, I was inspired. My goal was to leave here first-class. I remember reaching out to him multiple times on this deployment. Questioning how I could leave the ship online for the first class. I had a lot of hope.

20. I do not blame my LPO, Senior, or DivO because they cannot control the comments and behaviors of others. They do not know every single incident that takes place. They can only control so much. However, they did allow for things to get out of order by not addressing situations. They appeared more content to mediate the situation. Do they know which individuals are more receptive to change? They did move people; they did talk to people. They did do the bare minimum.

21. I believe the OI division needs order, discipline, and boundary lines. Professionalism and respect need to be addressed. The structural setup of who controls things needs to be re-established. Whenever our chain of command gives us an order, there should be no choice in the matter. Everything is too relaxed. Some people do their jobs and others don't. If the people who don't do their jobs are not being held accountable. Then, both behaviors are being ac. There is no perfect leader. Part of being a leader is being able to balance all the qualities. Being open to criticism. Having had my own a-way of doing things that is effective for the people you lead. Have a clear understanding of what is expected, tolerated, and valued amongst your people. Making them feel like they have a safe space. A chain of command whom they can trust. I completely understand that it is more easily said than done. Knowing what I now know, compared to two weeks ago, I think I have given a well-grasped and respectful summary of what is wrong with the OI division.

~ R. E. OZLYN ~

September 20th, 2021

Dear Diary,

Today is my early day. I came in at 5 am. I had a conversation with a fellow friend of mine. Then, I took a long nap and unwound.

The final words to my division:

Even though I am very disappointed in you all because you let me down. I let you down as well. I had hoped I could have made a difference better than the one I did. I tried so hard. I realize now that when I finally woke up from the heartache that I was going through, the little fire that had started all those months ago; had spread and was burning down the whole forest called our division. I tried multiple times to shine a light on everything. I think when I left the division, I was quiet for a moment. I was recovering from what had happened to me.

Here is the thing I have come to learn about people. Their behavior is a pattern and if you pay attention, you will learn to strike at the right moment. The other life skill I learned is that when people do things to hurt you, always find a way to be nice and nasty. You channel that bottled-up anger and turn it into something positive. You beat people at their own game. They will

> *The other life skill I learned is that when people do things to hurt you…*

171

start to burn from the inside out. When they went out of their way to continue doing the shenanigans that they've been doing, they set off a fire in me that burned to see a change within the division. I had something to say. I wrote that I wanted to help and make sure you all knew in the letter that there was a little OS3 who wanted nothing more than equality for all.

Someone who practiced what they preached and was not a hypocrite. Owned up to the cards of imperfection. A hard worker. I wanted to be a power team. I will never follow anyone into the fire. I think that is the worst way to die. You burn in agonizing pain for minutes. If seconds could feel like hours. Imagine how minutes could feel. I hope the change in the division comes sooner than later. I was promised the wrongs would be righted and I hope they are. I no longer talk to you all. Not because I don't want to. That is just how I am healing. I wish you all the best and I hope you all find what the future holds in store for you.

September 21st, 2021

Dear Diary,

Am I running away from something or toward something? No. I am not, nor will I ever run from something. What is meant to be will be. This was not meant to be. Xavier and I were not meant to be. I think I am finally accepting the concept of life. When you understand that things are not always in your control. Life would and could be so much better. The day I head home with my family, It will be joyous and marvelous. I am so excited, and October 6th could not come fast enough.

September 22nd, 2021

Dear Diary,

Today was pretty good. I am still working in S-2 until I leave. Seeing the CS1s since the situation was just awkward, and I know they don't like me anymore. It is not like I care because they were completely out of line. I handled the situation the best I could. I did a day's work. I worked on my letter. Earlier I sat with chaps, and I defused. Although I needed to share the letter because it's serious to me, it is true, I somehow feel not necessarily wrong about wanting to share it with the CO. But I never meant to disappoint CSCS by not coming to her about the situation in the first place. I just don't want to burn any bridges. My letter is spot on about how I feel and what is going on. I just want to handle this situation the best I can.

I've been thinking maybe I should share the letter with Senior. I should share the letter with my DivO. Maybe even Ops because I'm pretty sure he does not know what is going on. I don't want to make the wrong move. I just want to send a farewell in the right direction. I am going to start with CSCS and get her advice first.

I went to bible study tonight. The other night, I learned and became knowledgeable about a quote. Tonight, we watched a video and answered questions based on the video. The quote answered the question perfectly. The question was: what are the benefits of viewing life according to God's design versus mankind's execution of it?

I answered this question with the quote:

"Born twice and die one death and born once and die two deaths." Meaning we are born into the physical world. When we accept Christ as our savior, we are born again as Christians. We die a physical death, but we do not die a spiritual death. We live an eternal life in the kingdom of heaven. When we are born, we do not accept Christ, we die a physical death and a spiritual death. Forever burning in hell. Wow! I am so proud because my faith is not where it once was. This time I am building and planting my feet at the root of living a joyous life. By the Bible. I love the Bible. It is always true.

What problems do I expect from leaving my current ship? I do not know what to expect on my new ship. I am going in with an open mind. I cannot bring the problems I have with this command to another. I will go in more knowledgeable than before. I will try again and not make the same mistakes. Identify the Martha's, Diamond's, Xavier's, Max's, Fred's and everyone and anyone that is ruining my beautiful spirit. And stay the hell away!

On a serious note, I will not be guilty by association. When people think of me. I want them to have the right idea. I don't want a dark cloud constantly above me. I will not be grouped or paired with anyone. I will live my life like no other. I will wash away all the evil spirits and become a more proficient child of God. I will accept love and remove the hatred in my heart. I will heal properly. I will continue to strive for my dreams. I will be close to my family and true friends. No snakes or porch monkeys in sight. I will continue to surround myself with only good vibes. I will publish my book, join a church, and start boxing.

With so many aspirations, I cannot wait to start living for myself. I will continue to be honest and true to myself. I will continue to be myself. A kindhearted person and a joyous woman. I will continue to be human and make mistakes. I will also learn from those mistakes and grow even bigger.

My goal is to die one physical death and live eternally in the kingdom of heaven.

I didn't have to physically handle anything by myself. My enemies and haters struck themselves down. They are nonfactors. What God has in store for me, will continue to be in my life and be only for me.

September 23rd, 2021

Dear Diary,

Can I defend my choice to leave, even if others disagree? Yes. I can defend my choice because I live a life for myself and nobody else.

September 24th, 2021

Dear Diary,

Yesterday, I finally passed the board for an engineer with DCCS. I am so relieved. I did it. I completed my goal of getting my ESWS. I am so proud of myself. I just can't wait to get pinned. I am excited about that. Later that day, I also had a conversation. I had asked CSCS to set it up and I asked for it not to be up top. I don't like being up there. The letter that I wrote for the CO, I completed it on the 20th. The more that I read the letter, it was not a letter meant for the CO. I felt like it was meant for someone else. The last thing I would ever want to do is disrespect or blindside my chain of command. The letter did not exemplify a bad leadership style and who they were. I believed it was just a hard critique and it was something that came from the heart and was honest.

I felt so bad. I just felt like the best thing that could have said was, "they heard me." The fantastic news is they did hear me. I am so glad I was able to do something positive despite everything that I went through. When people try to hurt you, they only win if you let them. I did not let either one of them win. As much as I would love to punch them in the face. I wouldn't dare touch them. They don't know my purpose in life. I do.

What's my plan? My plan is the same. I am going to go to Florida and be the best that I can be. Being only in competition with myself. Not giving a care about either of these people. I will keep in touch with my Senior, IS1, and my friends. Like the CSS, QMs, and others. I am excited going forward. I made my mark in Virginia. Time for me to excel elsewhere.

September 25th, 2021

Dear Diary,

    I sent my letter off today. Am I scared? No. I am not scared of anyone or anything. The only thing I must fear is fear itself. I will continue to carry myself and be positive with good vibes. I will detach these evil spirits I've picked up. Or even the bad habits I've taken on without even knowing it. The world is mine for the taking. There is nothing either of these people can ever take from me. I will meet these people again. They will be non-factors. They will continue to live a life of selfishness. They will meet someone who is not nice or nasty as I am. They will suffer the consequences. Scared is one word I cannot relate to at this point in my life. I am grateful, ambitious, eager, excited, and almost any other word other than scared.

September 26th, 2021

Dear Diary, I wrote to Xavier...

    Dear Xavier,

If you truly did not want to be with me. Then, why did you accept what I had to offer?

    Answer: When I asked for the *Switch* back. It was a character test. I had mentioned multiple times prior that I had no desire for the *Switch*. Everything you asked me for, I have given it to you. I wanted to know if the one thing I asked you for were you going to do it for me. You failed. You didn't give me the *Switch* back. You called me an "Indian giver." You accepted what I had to offer because you are all of these people combined in one: a lying ass Max, slimy bitch like Martha, as dirty as Diamond, a groupie just like Fred, a womanizer just like Parker, a coward just like George, a want-to-be hoe like Pricilla, a little bitch like Stanley, a shit-starter like Earl, a hypocrite just like Reece, inconsiderate like Chrissy, petty like Larry and you are even more stupid than Wanda.

    You are all the people that I have grown to despise in one. You want to be like every one of them so badly. You know deep down they don't like you and they don't like themselves. In the end, I am one hundred percent certain you don't like them and you don't like yourself either. I accepted and forgave you for all that you were. Now that my sea goggles are off, I see you as a scared little boy. Correction! I see nothing. Don't get me wrong, you have all the potential to be a handsome man. I see the beautiful potential in everyone. It's up to them to live to be their full potential. A beautiful person to me is not skin deep. Even though some people are butt ugly. You are not ugly. However, beauty comes from within. At the core and embodied in the soul. Xavier, you are just an ugly person. I knew in Bahrain when we had a conversation.

You were a little drunk. I learned you a lot better than you think. I could tell you wanted to talk to me for weeks. You wanted me to hold you and be there for you. When you were telling me about your granddad that passed away. I wanted to feel sorry for you. My heart and my head read the situation completely differently. My heart loves you and will always love you for some weird reason. My head said, "I don't know if he wanted a pillow, but I ain't it." I thought you deserved everything that was coming your way. Not to mention that you put our business out to everyone. You made your bed and you got to lie in it. I didn't feel sorry for you.

I felt sorry for myself. What the hell was I thinking? I am way out of your league. I see you crying like the first time we bonded. We were bonding, and you told me you did "things" with your guy best friend. It was the thing you were most ashamed of.

The more I think of how you chose Pricilla over me. The more I thought you were gay. There is nothing wrong with that. I wanted to hurt you the way you hurt me. You even went as low as sharing the personal conversations you and I had with them. That posse you so desperately wanted to fit into. In addition to bringing up the darkest secret I told you in private, you chose all those people who didn't care about you over me. I tried to warn you. In Bahrain, there you were begging for me to be that version of myself that you tried so hard to destroy. You did destroy the version of me you had access to. You could never and would never destroy me. You ruined one of the best things that came into your life.

I am so excited you let me go. When I finally stopped and let you go. You came back. What you forgot was you let me go first. I could and would never go back to you, Xavier. Not back to somebody who is so weak-minded. So easily intimidated. A weak, spineless follower. Someone so ugly inside and out. So alone and damaged that you choose pain over genuine love. That is something you must deal with by yourself. I meant the last thing I said to you. "Don't talk to me!" In combat when you stopped talking to me, that hurt me so badly. I picked up my pride and I left. I hope you live the life that best serves you. I would not be surprised if you ended up just like the rest of them. Alone, afraid, and unloved.

September 27th, 2021

Dear Diary,

Yesterday, they had a photo taken for supply. Today, they had a photo taken for operations. I partook in neither photo. The reason for not being in the operations photo was I didn't feel well. I no longer want to be involved with that division. That could have been my family, but they aren't. They never were. I am perfectly okay with that. Those people are like vultures. They feed on the dead. I live too well to ever be mistaken for dead. Not now and not ever. As much as I have grown to despise them. I wish them luck. I give them my best wishes that they live the life they deserve. I have always been that kind of person.

Where I learned to love people from a distance. It's like every time I visit my family. The first three days are great. I miss them. We laugh, hug, and love one another. Then, by the fourth day, I got to go. Things start to fall apart and we need that distance again. I don't consider it a bad thing. I think it is just "life." When we are young, we are forced to be around people. That is why children rebel at certain ages. As we get older, we pick and choose. I don't choose these people. I did my best to help in the best way that I could. I hope the division thrives.

I have one week left in this place. I am so happy. Can't wait to eat some real food and start heading home. I hope my orders say Florida. That's my focus.

September 28th, 2021

Dear Diary, I wrote to Senior...

Dear Senior,

You are a phenomenal leader. I would not have chosen differently in any other lifetime. The valued lessons and life skills I have learned from being your sailor will live with me forever. I wanted to clarify and mention this to you. I do not fault you for anything. I acknowledge the fact that you are human. As humans, we make mistakes. I commend you for responding to me the way you did in terms of being approachable and open-minded. Taking ownership. Above all, for being like a second father to me.

In life, we meet people for one of two reasons. Either a lesson or a blessing. You are indeed a wonderful blessing. I may never and could never have a chief/senior like you ever again. You are highly favored and will forever be in my memory. I do not blame you for my true feelings toward the division.

I do not blame you for Parker attacking me. I don't blame you for anything. I just want to shine a light on the greater potential that lives in you and be that wonderful blessing in disguise.

I am glad a letter can go a long way. I am slowly learning my true purpose for being on this earth. As a Christian. As a strong black woman. As a sailor. As an OS and every other title, I pick up towards the end of my lifetime. When I was at my lowest, I had a conversation and laid all the cards on the table. You were there to help pick me up in my time of need. I will forever be appreciative. After that conversation, I knew I could never let you down. I had to pick myself up and get it together. Not just for you but for myself. I didn't know back then that I had to lift my head and fulfill one of the purposes god had in store for me. I am glad I was able to help. It was an absolute pleasure serving under Big Chief and to witness the beginnings of a gracious senior.

Very Respectfully,

Da-Da-Oh!

September 29th, 2021

Dear Diary, I wrote to my best friend...

Dear Best Friend,

Where to begin? You have become my best friend for so many reasons. I remember the first time we hung out together. We decided to go to iHop before we went to the club. We were in the booth, talking and laughing. The waiter came up and asked, "Are you two best friends?" I thought, "Wow, that's different." Now I know that was spoken into existence. I have grown to love you so freaking much, love you to the moon and back. The way you have the same values and outlook on life is awesome. We are strong and fierce. We are the future.

I want to forever thank you for being that listening ear when my world fell apart on February 22. You are one of the greatest blessings I have ever received. I had two previous best friends at different periods in my life.

My first best friend was around fourth grade. I was there for her, but when I needed her to have my back, she never was there. These two black girls were trying to fight her. I stood up for her. I supported her. She somehow pinned things on me. Somehow guys liked her, and they would throw me under the bus to protect a conniving devil. I didn't even do the things they spoke of, but the fingers were pointed at me. Later in life, I became a part of friend groups. I would think that I was close to someone. No, I was mistaken. They were a lot closer to someone else. I would feel bad because I felt stupid. I was thinking that's a bummer. I had another best friend.

We became best friends when I was working at Walgreens at 16 years old. We fell out because she was fake to me. She talked about not being friends with this girl. Behind my back, she was hanging out and becoming friends with me. Then, she just smiled at my face and acted like there was nothing wrong with that. If it wasn't clear, I didn't like the other girl. We fell out and we weren't friends after that. Both of my best friends stabbed me in the back.

In addition, whenever I shared the specifics and the incidents with my mom and auntie, they always beat it into me. You don't have friends. You have associates. Learning what I know now, I agree and disagree with them. I have friends, just those who were not my friends. None of them had the potential to be my best friends.

Now I know there are two different types of friendships. There are situational friendships and there are real friendships. Situational friends are people whom you are forced to be around for school, work, sports, etc. If it wasn't for a forced setting, you most likely wouldn't be friends with them.

True Friends are friends that could be situational in the beginning. How do you know they are true? They reach out and comfort you when needed. They have your best interest at heart. They are honest and they can be trusted. They are there with you through thick and thin as a support system. I only have a few true friends. Now I only have one best friend. I waited all this time for someone who is truly and will forever be with me in my time of need. I love you. I am forever grateful. I cannot stress enough. If it wasn't clear, you have my love and support to the end of time. Sisters for life.

Sincerely,

Your Best Friend.

September 30th, 2021

Dear Diary, I wrote to Chaps…

Dear Chaps,

I know it is your job to help us. I know you are a genuine person. I also know I thanked you several times and the truth is, I cannot thank you enough. Every time I needed a voice to listen to and confide in. You were it. I don't like people to see me cry. I bet you have seen more tears on my face than you can count. You were a blessing and our conversation will forever be in my memories. I am so proud that I made it because you were one of the few that reassured me of my sanity. I learned so much from you.

My spirit has grown so much as well. I can never forget the first conversation I had with you. It was sometime in October 2020. When I had all of that emotional weight on me. It was so heavy that it felt physical and it was weighing down on my heart. After I was completely honest, you told me that some people are like mosquitoes. They latch on and suck all the blood right out of you. If you let them, they will drain you dry. When did you realize you have a mosquito on you? You have to kill it, figuratively speaking. That was about a friendship I had to let go of. You helped me see that. You opened my eyes to a lot about people, the bible and God.

I know I questioned the plan in store for me. You reassured me and kept drilling in me that I have to keep the faith. I will and I do. I learned about the Father, the Son, and the Holy Spirit in your bible studies.

Very Respectfully,

-Little Sis.

October 1st, 2021

Dear Diary,

Today was a long day. We are in a drill for the next couple of days. It is so draining. After yesterday's little mishap, I want to punch that bitch in her face so badly. A two-for-one special. I can't. I don't want to focus on that. Today I started my checkout sheet. I am so glad that I am leaving. Hopefully, I get my orders tomorrow and it says Florida. I have decided that I am going to be a great author. I am. I have a lot of anger, and I am going to channel that anger into something positive. I made a promise that I wouldn't fight or cuss anyone out. I would just walk away.

Because of the internet, I have not been able to log onto school. I was able to log in today. Of course, we are going through a hurricane. The rocking just makes me a little uneasy.

My New Rules for Being in the Military:

1. Guilty by Association
2. Take accountability
3. Do not shit where you eat
4. Don't be afraid to be alone (self-love is key)
5. Live life for yourself first

6. Let them underestimate; just don't disappoint
7. Find people on your level
8. Live a life with no regrets
9. Never apologize
10. Compromise never sympathizes

October 3rd, 2021

Dear Diary,

Today I got pinned for my ESWS. I am so proud. OS3 (SW), that's me. I am beyond proud. I know I was being petty today. As much as I want to punch them girls in their faces. I know and am beyond aware that it is wrong to do it. These girls have no respect for themselves or anybody else. All these vultures are just looking for gossip and a quick sexual encounter. I am so glad that I am leaving and getting a new beginning. I talked to this BM2. I talked to him from time to time. I thought he was cool. Now, I am starting to learn about people. I am starting to get to know these people.

After Parker attacked me, the biggest message and advice I was getting was the steps I should have taken to prevent it. Are they serious? Parker was out of control. He should not have been putting his hands on people to begin with. If you know you have a drinking problem, try not to drink. Maybe that would work? Do you mean to tell me that after six victims later, Parker isn't the problem? I am still the problem.

My bad seven, including the female on his last ship. Correction! Eight victims, including his wife. BM2 and anybody else can keep that advice to themselves. I don't want it. I am going to live my life the way that I want. Roaming the ship and doing my job. If they can roam the ship with no one putting their hands on them, so can I; either they handle them, or I will. If anyone puts their hands on me, I am going to defend myself.

October 4th, 2021

Dear Diary,

Today, I got my orders, and it says Florida. I am so excited. I can thank nobody else other than the Lord himself. I want to confess. It is slowly not bothering me the opinions that these people on my first platform have about me. It is amazing the lies they tell one another or even the topics of conversation. My nana always told me, "Opinions are like assholes and everybody has one."

If I spent every day thinking about other people's assholes, contemplating about what color their feces is? Or even the disgusting smell their asses make when they go to the bathroom, that would be so nasty and disgusting. That would be like caring about their opinions. These people are disgusting. I don't care what they have to say about me. Let them talk because, most likely, they are spreading lies.

October 5th, 2021

Dear Diary, I wrote to my mentor...

Dear Mentor,

I remember when you said. "We are going to make it through this deployment. You are going to see it. "You were right because we did. All the trials and tribulations. We made it. I'm glad you saw the future because I didn't. You were my mentor before deployment, but when you helped pick me up from a dark place. That was something a beautiful person would do. I am so proud of myself. I am proud of you.

Oftentimes people wish for happiness. People fail to realize that happiness is temporary, and joy is everlasting. I wish you a lifetime of joy. I pray that your family stays blessed and you live a joyous life. We shared so much, and we picked each other up. I never had a mentor that stuck it out with me for the long haul. They were only there for the season. You are the real deal. I know there is another promotion in store for you. I keep you in my prayers and I use your lessons daily. I thank you for my first devotional. It helped me to learn more about the bible. It gave me the extra boost that I needed in my spirit and I thank you from one child of God to another.

Very Respectfully,

~ A Mini You ~

Chapter 10: Food For Thought

Dear Diary,

I wish my DivO would have played her role way better than she did. I believe that my divo went back and told them things that she shouldn't. There is nothing that anybody can tell me to convince me differently. Swing how CTT1 and GM1 knew things, but they played stupid. With my DivO, I could see the guilt in her eyes when I was on shore duty and she tried to have a conversation with me.

GM1 was sitting there observing everything; I felt like at the end of every conversation, I was talking to a brick wall. She was Max's mentor. Of course, she's not willing to see everything for what it was. She was also up for chief, so of course, she wasn't willing to look past both the CS1 and what they were doing. I know she kept trying to tell me. "You won Oz. You are not leaving quietly and things are changing." What could you possibly tell me that I won? I didn't think it would have to be a big event for things to change. I can't sit and have a good mentality towards anybody in that division. There is nothing none of them can say to me to make me think differently.

They are CS1 and they are twice our age. They are preying on us. If that's not some pedophilic shit, I don't know what is because in my perspective, when we were in the womb, or perhaps 1, 2, or 3 years of age, they were the age that we are right now. We literally could be the age of their kids. The fact that the conversation asked, "oh, who's easy? Would you judge me if I did anything with Diamond?" That is so disgusting.

How do you live with yourself? How do you look at your kids and then go prey on the kids that could be your kids? Imagine if your kids were being preyed on by someone just like you. Fuck all that gym shit. Or I'll kill somebody bout my kid's mentality. I would never look at them the same. Because before they put on that collar device, they were human first. Although one of them spoke. He spoke for both of them. They didn't care, so I don't give a fuck either. Respect is earned. It's not given. When they failed to respect me. I lost all respect for both of the CS1s.

Chastising others but being friends with the people who cause problems.

If you are mad at my honest opinion and summary of you, then maybe you should reconsider the perception and opinion you present to people.

Maybe you should rethink your behavior and actions going forward. Or you can continue and behave as you see fit. I don't care.

I find it hard to believe that my chain of command did not know about the situations that happened under their nose. Furthermore, they did nothing about the situations that they were aware of. I find it hard to believe that they couldn't do anything about it. Okay, if they didn't know. How could they not be aware of something so serious going on in their division? I do not understand the logic.

Parker went off on his rant before the incident. He mentioned the thing I told Xavier in private. Meaning everybody knew something, but nobody filled me in. Ozlyn's feelings were never validated and nobody gave a fuck. I am so fucking angry with these people. I hate their fucking guts. I could have blacked out and done the worst to these motherfuckers.

That explains why Parker said, "you telling my wife this, that and the third."

What specifically is this, that and the third? What is it? What person, place, or situation did I tell Deborah about? What I told her was vague as fuck and I clarified to her stupid ass that I stopped hanging around Parker. I didn't know anything for sure. Verbatim, what I told Deborah was," everything I heard was hearsay and it all just sounded like guilty behavior to me." That is what I said, exactly. I didn't give her any names, no incidents, and no conversations. Either Deborah or Parker was trying to put words in my mouth. I am not a dummy. I tried, but these people just don't deserve me or my time.

> I tried, but these people just don't deserve me or my time.

It's not my fault that they don't have anything on me. They wish they did because what did I do to either one of them: Xavier, Martha, Max, Parker, Deborah, George, Diamond, Earl? What did I do to them for them to have animosity towards me?

Diamond and Martha both thought what happened to me was funny. They were all joking with the group, including Xavier.

I know Xavier is thinking he's gonna get stationed in California and shit is going to be all sweet and nice. No, fuck that! I want to blow this story up. Since they all want to put me in a filthy spotlight. Well, I'm gonna steal the whole mother fuckin show.

You don't get to hurt people and tell them when and how to heal. You can't do all three.

I read the book about the five love languages. Xavier and I spoke two different love languages. Xavier's love language is quality time. That's why he spent all his time with me for six months. He gave me back massages, double-checked on me and wanted to know every detail about me.

My love language is actions. I showed my love for him through my actions. I was there for him, supported and accepted him for all that he was. To me, actions speak louder than words. That's why we agreed to talk and give it time. I wanted him just as much as he wanted me. I think we fell in love with each other, but I know Xavier would never admit that he loves me. When he did what he did, he knew he crossed the point of no return.

I stopped speaking his love language and he stopped speaking mine. I think it was easier for him to continue with something he didn't want. Priscilla was easier. It was easier for him to make a fool of himself with her.

Maybe in a sick fantasy, he was even trying to punish himself with her. He knew he could never be with me again. So, why would he not stick with the leftovers? It was something rather than nothing to him.

His eyes told the full story. It was the toxic and narcissistic behavior he showed me. I couldn't and I wouldn't go back to him. Even if we were love at first sight. Even if we were soulmates. Even if the chemistry between us was dying to attract.

I heard this guy on TikTok say, "The thing about opposites is that they don't attract for long. Eventually, they repel." No matter how much I truly didn't want to let Xavier go. I had to. Since he denied my feelings and me. I guess it's safe to say I fell in love with someone who never existed.

Last Diary Entry

"I used to think I was naive about the world, but now I know the world is just naive about me."

I used to think I
was naive about
the world…

~ RSE ~

Dear Diary,

This is a quote from an old friend of mine. She and I go way back. She is such a huge inspiration. Without her help, I would have never been able to tell my story. She is a fantastic person and a great friend out of all the "friends" I've made in the last few years. She has been the most loyal, reliable, and strongest friend I have ever had. I owe her a lot of respect. She and I see eye to eye and we can relate like no other. I have always stated I wish I had a friend that was more like myself in the past. That was imperfectly perfect and had such an awesome character and spiritual energy.

This is the end of this book. I don't plan on sharing any more of my diary entries ever again. I don't plan on writing a book about my new command. I think this book can help anyone going on deployment, anyone who is going through heartache, or just a tough time. This book can hopefully give you some humor. Uplift someone from any walk of life. I want to share my story.

I completed my first deployment dealing with so many storms. Can you imagine being out in the middle of the ocean fighting for our nation and simultaneously trying to stay sane? While also being cut off from friends and family and the world for periods at a time. I was trying so hard to heal in an environment that was not good for me. Overcoming people who were toxic to me. Overcoming enemies. Being assaulted by someone so much of a friend to me, he called me his little sister. You can do whatever it is you are trying to do.

I want to confess. The incident with Parker dulled my motivation a bit. I am like six weeks behind on classes. All the plans that I had were rearranged, and I elaborated on all the things that I felt were unfair. At the end of each beautiful day, I can "only focus on what I can control." The quote Captain instilled into everyone on board. Now I am refocused. I can control working on my classes toward my bachelor's. I can control my finances and finance myself with a new car. I can control the people I allow in my inner circle. I can control the distance I put between my family and myself. I can control my reactions. Everything that happened at my first command did not, would not, could not and will never stop me from pursuing my dreams in my life.

I love this question I found on YouTube. Can you kill an alligator with your bare hands?

Answer: I added this question at the back of the book because I watched a video on it. Once an alligator has his eyes set on his prey, he is focused and he strikes at the right moment. However, after the alligator eats his dinner and he falls into a paralyzed state. That is the moment the alligator is most vulnerable, and you can strike and kill the alligator.

About humans. If you have a goal and you obtain it. Just because you have had a taste of a little success, are you going to stop and become paralyzed in a sense? Or are you going to stay vigilant and keep hunting? At the end of the video, he said, "I ask the question again, can you kill an alligator with your bare hands?

"My answer is yes, I can. I don't know where it comes from. I guess it is just in me, but I keep hustling. I keep striving. I have plans, and I am going to take the world over. Goal after goal. Nobody can ever hold me back. No one can stop me. Not even people who pray for my downfall. I am a daughter of God. That is my shield of protection. I am untouchable in a sense. These people tried to break me. They couldn't. I'm stronger. I'm wiser. They have no idea. That even if I am full right now. I'm not going to stop. I'm going to keep charging. I always have room for dessert.

When my ship arrived for homecoming, my family was the loudest crowd out on the pier. We heard them from a mile away. It was the warmest feeling ever. After homecoming, the only thing I could do was smile from ear to ear. I went back to the hotel room with my family. I ended up going out to a club with my best friend. Her husband Richard, who is also Xavier's best friend, told me that he was "really sorry for everything." Aww! I know, really sweet. I think not. I took a mental note of the message that was passed on to me. When I went out to the club later that night, I texted Xavier and said I accepted his apology. I only sent him that text message to truly show the strength the Lord has given me.

With the character and the pure heart that I am blessed to have, I do not need nor want Xavier's apology. Whatever bull shit story he needs to tell himself to fall asleep at night. It is between him and his demons. Xavier is in denial. It is amazing how he still hangs on to his lies. At least he still has a conscience, and he feels guilty. This is why he feels the need to apologize.

If you know in your heart that you truly didn't do anything wrong. Why would you apologize? I don't feel guilty about any of my actions. I didn't do anything wrong to either of them. If I did, it was when they were trying to gang up on me and back me into a corner. I'm telling my story one way or another. I do not feel guilty about anything that I shared in my book and I am not sorry.

www.ingramcontent.com/pod-product-compliance
Lightning Source LLC
Chambersburg PA
CBHW071330120626
46546CB00002B/515